EFFECTS OF INUNDATION ON CULTURAL RESOURCES

IN PAINTED ROCK RESERVOIR, ARIZONA

An Assessment

by

David A. Phillips, Jr.

and Kenneth Rozen

Submitted by

Cultural Resource Management Division

Arizona State Museum

University of Arizona

to

The U.S. Army Corps of Engineers

Los Angeles District

P.O. Number SPLED-EP-81-3802

April 1982

Archaeological Series Number 14

CONTENTS

FIGURES   ix

TABLES   xi

ABSTRACT   xiii

ACKNOWLEDGMENTS   xv

NOTICE   xv

CHAPTER
  1. INTRODUCTION   1

  2. NATURAL AND CULTURAL SETTING   3
      Environment   3
      Cultural History   5
          Preceramic Period   5
          Ceramic Period   6
          Historic Period   6

  3. SURVEY METHODS   9
      Study of Aerial Photographs   9
      Limits of Survey   9
      Intensity of Coverage   10
      Site Definition and Records   10
      Collections   11

  4. SURVEY RESULTS   13
      Site Descriptions   13
          AZ T:13:22 (PRS-78-16; PRI-1; "Rock City")   13
              Features   14
                  Feature 1   14
                  Feature 2   14
                  Feature 3   17
                  Feature 4   17
                  Feature 5   17
                  Feature 6   17
                  Feature 8   19
                  Feature 10   19
                  Feature 11   19
                  Feature 13   21
                  Feature 14   21
                  Feature 15   21

Feature 16   21
Feature 17A   21
Feature 17B   24
Feature 20   24
Feature 22A   24
Feature 22B   27
Feature 23   27
Feature 24   27
Feature 26   31
Feature 28A   31
Feature 28B   31
Feature 29   31
Feature 30   33
Feature 33   33
Feature 34   33
Feature 35A   36
Feature 35B   36
Feature 36   36
Feature 37   36
Feature 38   37
Feature 39   37
Feature 40   37
Feature 41   37
Feature 42   40
Feature 43   40
Feature 44   40
Feature 45   40
Feature 46   43
Feature 47   43
Feature 48   43
Feature 50   43
Trails   47
Other Artifacts   47
AZ T:13:22: Concluding Comments   47
AZ T:13:23 (PRI-4)   47
Description of Remains   49
Feature 1   49
Feature 2   49
Feature 3   49
Feature 4   49
Feature 5   49
Trail   49
Other Remains   51
Inundation Effects   51
AZ T:13:24 (PRI-6)   51
Description of Remains   51
Feature 1   51
Feature 2   51
Feature 3   51
Feature 4   53
Feature 5   53
Feature 6   53

Contents   v

Feature 7	53
Feature 8	53
Feature 9	53
Feature 10	53
Feature 11	54
Feature 12	54
Inundation Effects	54
AZ T:13:25 (PRI-9)	54
AZ T:13:26 (PRI-12)	54
AZ T:13:27 (PRI-23)	57
AZ T:13:28 (PRI-43)	57
AZ T:13:29 (PRI-63)	60
AZ T:13:30 (PRS-78-22)	60
Features	64
Trail	64
Petroglyphs	64
Artifacts	64
Disturbance	65
AZ T:13:31 (PRS-78-23)	65
Other Finds	69
PRI-2	69
PRI-3	69
PRI-5	69
PRI-7	69
PRI-8	69
PRI-10	70
PRI-11	70
PRI-13	70
PRI-14	70
PRI-15	70
PRI-16	73
PRI-17	73
PRI-18	73
PRI-19	73
PRI-20	73
PRI-21	73
PRI-22	73
PRI-24	74
PRI-25	74
PRI-26	74
PRI-27	74
PRI-28	77
PRI-29	77
PRI-30	77
PRI-31	77
PRI-32	77
PRI-33	79
PRI-34	79
PRI-35	79
PRI-36	79
PRI-37	79
PRI-38	81

PRI-39   81
PRI-40   81
PRI-41   81
PRI-42   81
PRI-44   81
PRI-45   81
PRI-46   82
PRI-47   82
PRI-48   82
PRI-49   82
PRI-50   82
PRI-51   82
PRI-52   82
PRI-53   83
PRI-54   83
PRI-55   83
PRI-56   83
PRI-57   83
PRI-58   83
PRI-59   83
PRI-60   84
PRI-61   84
PRI-62   84
PRI-64   84
PRI-65   84
PRI-66   84
PRI-67   84
PRI-68   85
PRI-69   85
PRI-70   85
PRI-71   85
PRI-72   85
PRI-73   85
PRI-74   85
PRI-75   85
PRI-76   86
PRI-77   86
PRI-78   86
PRI-79   86
PRI-80   86
Other Trails   86
Survey Results: A Brief Interpretation   88

5. AGE, SIGNIFICANCE, AND
    NATIONAL REGISTER ELIGIBILITY OF REMAINS   91
      Age of the Finds   91
      Significance of the Finds   98
        Recent Remains   98
        Ambiguous Remains   98
        Early Remains   98
      Eligibility for the National Register   99

6. RECOMMENDATIONS AND CONCLUSIONS   101
      Effects of Inundation: Some General Comments   101
      Specific Recommendations   110

APPENDIX A Cultural Resources Locational Data   113

APPENDIX B Standard ASM Site Form and "Short Form"   119

APPENDIX C Mitigation Program for Study Area   135

APPENDIX D Collections   141

REFERENCES   143

FIGURES

4.1   AZ T:13:22, Features 1, 36, and 37   15
4.2   AZ T:13:22, Features 2, 3, and 6   16
4.3   AZ T:13:22, Features 4, 5, and 8   18
4.4   AZ T:13:22, Features 10 and 11   20
4.5   AZ T:13:22, Features 13, 14, 15, and 16   22
4.6   AZ T:13:22, Features 17A and 17B   23
4.7   AZ T:13:22, Features 20 and 22B   25
4.8   AZ T:13:22, Features 22A, 29, 33, and 35A   26
4.9   AZ T:13:22, Feature 23   28
4.10   AZ T:13:22, Feature 23 before inundation   29
4.11   AZ T:13:22, Feature 23 after inundation   29
4.12   AZ T:13:22, Features 24, 26, 42, and 43   30
4.13   AZ T:13:22, Features 28A, 28B, 30, and 44   32
4.14   AZ T:13:22, Feature 29 before inundation   34
4.15   AZ T:13:22, Feature 29 after inundation   34
4.16   AZ T:13:22, Features 34 and 35B   35
4.17   AZ T:13:22, Features 38, 39, 41, and 45   38
4.18   AZ T:13:22, Feature 40   39
4.19   AZ T:13:22, Feature 42 before inundation   41
4.20   AZ T:13:22, Feature 42 after inundation   41
4.21   AZ T:13:22, Feature 44 before inundation   42
4.22   AZ T:13:22, Feature 44 after inundation   42
4.23   AZ T:13:22, Features 46, 47, 48, and 50   44
4.24   AZ T:13:22, Feature 47 before inundation   45
4.25   AZ T:13:22, Feature 47 after inundation   45
4.26   AZ T:13:22, Feature 50 before inundation   46
4.27   AZ T:13:22, Feature 50 after inundation   46
4.28   AZ T:13:23   48
4.29   AZ T:13:23, petroglyph   50
4.30   AZ T:13:30, Feature 6, petroglyph   50
4.31   AZ T:13:24 and AZ T:13:25; PRI-51 and PRI-52   52
4.32   AZ T;13:25, detail map of rock ring   55
4.33   AZ T:13:26   56
4.34   AZ T:13:27   58
4.35   AZ T:13:28   59
4.36   AZ T:13:29   61
4.37   AZ T:13:30 and AZ T:13:31; PRI-25, 26, 32 and 33   62
4.38   AZ T:13:30   63
4.39   AZ T:13:31   66
4.40   AZ T:13:31 and study area from AZ T:13:30   67
4.41   AZ T:13:31 after inundation   67
4.42   AZ T:13:31, Feature 1 before inundation   68
4.43   AZ T:13:31, Feature 1 after inundation   68

x Figures

4.44   PRI-10, 16, 19 and 20   71
4.45   PRI-11 and PRI-22   72
4.46   PRI-24, 27, 28 and 29   75
4.47   PRI-26 and PRI-30   76
4.48   PRI-32   78
4.49   PRI-33, 34, 45, and 46   80
A.1   Locations of sites   117
A.2   Trails in the study area   118
Map 1 (in pocket)

TABLES

5.1   Distribution of enclosures by style   93
5.2   Distribution of enclosures relative to labor camp   94
5.3   Enclosure characteristics relative to location   95
5.4   Distribution of large rectangular
        versus other enclosures   96
6.1   Cultural resources: extent, type
        condition, and recommendations   102

xi

ABSTRACT

In August 1981 the Cultural Resource Management Division of the
Arizona State Museum carried out a 640-acre archaeological survey at
Painted Rock Dam in southwestern Arizona. The study, sponsored by the
Los Angeles District of the U.S. Army Corps of Engineers, assessed the
effects of inundation on rock alignments and other remains.

Intensive survey revealed 82 finds in or near the study area,
ranging from isolated artifacts to "Rock City," a complex of trails,
rock alignments, and artifacts. The remains range in age from probably
Preceramic to Recent, but in many cases the actual age and cultural
affiliation of finds were ambiguous. This report attempts to
distinguish ancient from recent alignments and assesses the potential
significance of the remains.

Ability to assess the effects of inundation was limited by the
lack of pre-inundation data. Nonetheless, some conclusions were
reached. Inundation damage was largely due to wave action and was most
pronounced on slopes and on top of ridges or knolls. Wave action could
ultimately destroy all sites within the reservoir area, but the rate of
destruction is unknown and will vary according to the physical setting
of sites. The report ends with recommendations for a program of site
monitoring and testing and excavation of sites in immediate danger.

ACKNOWLEDGMENTS

Special thanks go to our fellow crew members, Annick George and Deni Seymour, each of whom bore a week of triple-digit temperatures with good cheer. We are also indebted to those who helped back at the Museum: Ray Pers, who charged into the red tape for us; Brian Byrd, who spent many hours drafting our map and illustrations; Bruce Huckell, who identified our collection; Jon Czaplicki and Lynn Teague, for input and critical comments; Maria Abdin, who typed a chunk of the report on short notice; and Rose Houk and Ben Smith, who edited the report for us. To these people and all the others who helped, thanks.

NOTICE

Appendix A contains locational data for archaeological sites. To protect the sites from possible vandalism, any copy of this report intended for unrestricted distribution should not include Appendix A.

Chapter 1

INTRODUCTION

This report describes research done at Painted Rock Dam, Arizona, under P.O. No. SPLED-EP-81-3802, for the U.S. Army Corps of Engineers, Los Angeles District. The purpose of the study was to assess inundation effects on sites within a 2.6-sq-km (640-acre) area.

Painted Rock Dam, completed in 1959, is designed to control floods along the lower Gila River. The dam is about 29 km (18 miles) northwest of the town of Gila Bend, in a Basin and Range setting marked by desert plant life. Its reservoir would flood about 214 sq km (53,000 acres) at spillway crest (661 feet above MSL) (Corps of Engineers 1975: A-1), but pool size varies greatly.

The reservoir area contains a number of recorded archaeological sites (Vogler 1975; Teague and Baldwin 1978). Others, no doubt, remain to be found. The Corps of Engineers is involved in the protection, recovery, and preservation of these cultural resources under various federal laws and policies (Vogler 1975: 3-9).

In 1978, the Arizona State Museum surveyed a 10-percent sample of the reservoir area (Teague and Baldwin 1978). Among the sites found were PRS-78-16, PRS-78-22, and PRS-78-23, which lie within a mile of each other. The Corps of Engineers later studied aerial photographs of this location and concluded that a number of rock alignments and trails existed in the vicinity.

In August 1981 a crew from the Cultural Resource Management Division spent 11 days locating and recording sites within the project area. The crew consisted of David Phillips as field supervisor, and Ken Rozen, Annick George, and Deni Seymour as field assistants. In addition, Vea Ltd. of Tucson mapped several sites. A total of 45 person-days was spent in the field. Report preparation involved the efforts of Lynn Teague (Principal Investigator), Jon Czaplicki (Project Director), David Phillips (Project Archaeologist), and Kenneth Rozen (crew member) over five weeks.

Chapter 2

NATURAL AND CULTURAL SETTING

Environment

Painted Rock Dam sits athwart the Gila River near the town of
Gila Bend in southwestern Arizona. If full, the dam's reservoir would
cover much of the great southward loop made by the Gila as it flows
around the Gila Bend Mountains. The area is part of the Sonoran Basin
and Range province, in which abrupt mountains alternate with broad,
sloping aprons of outwash gravels and alluvium. The study area proper
includes portions of the Gila floodplain, the low terrace or terraces
immediately next to it, and an expanse of open desert atop a low mesa or
bluff.

The area's appearance has probably changed greatly since the end
of the Pleistocene (Van Devender 1977). At that time in southwestern
Arizona pinyon trees grew as low as 510 m (1670 feet), and juniper could
be found at elevations down to 260 m (850 feet). Evidence for a
creosote-bur sage community was found at 160 m (525 feet) near Yuma, but
palo verde and saguaro probably were absent. Joshua trees, live oak,
and sagebrush may have been present. Modern desertscrub communities
probably did not form until about 6000 B.C. (Van Devender 1977: 190-191)
and have been relatively stable since then (Martin 1963).

One environmental change directly relevant to this study is the
formation of malpais (rock and boulder-strewn surfaces), which
presumably took place since the end of the Pleistocene. Many remains
found during this study are located in malpais, indicating that they
postdate the formation of these surfaces. Geological dating of this
process(es) would, therefore, indicate the maximum possible age of the
remains that were found.

Today, the region is hot and dry. Annual rainfall at Gila Bend
averages 145 mm (5.7 inches), with summer and winter peaks. Mean annual
temperature is 22 degrees Centigrade (72 degrees F), with mean maximum
and minimum temperatures of 42 and 2 degrees Centigrade (108 and 36
degrees F). There are about 344 frost-free days each year (Vogler 1975:
10).

Until recently, the study area was dominated by a creosote-bur
sage community (a desertscrub formation of the Lower Colorado Valley
province, Lower Sonoran Life Zone) (Brown and Lowe 1974). While bur
sage was present, the tendency was toward almost pure associations of
creosote bush. Palo verde, saguaro, and cholla were present and

3

associated on slopes and along drainages, but not to the exclusion of creosote bush. Animal life included mule deer, jack rabbits, cottontails, rodents, other mammals, and a variety of birds, reptiles, and amphibians (Corps of Engineers 1975).

Despite the summer heat, the region surrounding the study area must have been highly attractive to native peoples. Until about 1870 the Gila was a permanent river with rich plant and animal life. It would have enticed waterfowl and contained fish, and irrigation farming (with double-cropping) or floodwater farming would have been possible. The Gila once supported marshes and an extensive mesquite bosque (Lowe 1964: 29-30). The bosque, especially, would have attracted ancient peoples, since the mesquite pods could have been used as a dietary staple. (Part of the study area lies within this floodplain, but its original plant cover is unknown.) Land outside the floodplain could have been used for gathering cactus fruits and for hunting.

In the last hundred years, Anglo-American control of the region has radically altered the natural setting. Heavy water use and dam construction farther upriver have reduced the Gila to an intermittent stream. Old land surfaces have been destroyed by grading to permit uniform fields for irrigation. Within the study area, one such field was built on the Gila floodplain; land nearby was similarly leveled to provide space for a labor camp. A dike protected the field and camp from runoff; enough moisture collected behind the dike to encourage mesquite (?) and possibly salt cedar to grow. A graded road, two power lines, and partly-bladed jeep trails crossed the study area. Finally, heavy cattle grazing probably resulted in the sparse grasses evident today. Nonetheless, until recently most of the study area bore some resemblance to its original, natural state.

In 1973, trapped floodwaters encroached on the study area for the first time. Since then, several episodes of flooding have taken place, with a maximum pool height of 647.8 feet in March 1980. Within the flooded areas, native plant life was drowned and replaced by dense, almost unbroken salt cedar: in August 1981 this species accounted for about 99 percent of plant cover below flood line. Plants ranged from 0.5 m to about 3 m in height. Remaining plants were a variety of species apparently introduced by the floodwaters: these included saltbush, a number of unidentified weedy annuals, and one example of the striking but highly toxic tree tobacco. Except for nighthawks, doves, and snakes, animals were rare. Inundation effects will be discussed further in later chapters.

Cultural History

Preceramic Period

Humans have been in the Southwest for at least 10,000 years, but there is little evidence of them at Painted Rock before about A.D. 500. We believe that some of the remains we found may be Preceramic, so we will discuss this period. It is possible to use results from other areas (Irwin-Williams 1979, Warren 1967, Wallace 1978) to anticipate what was found at Painted Rock. The comments that follow, however, describe regional trends that may or may not prove applicable to Painted Rock.

From about 10,000 to 6000 B.C., the Gila Bend area was probably used by "hunting" groups. Sites of this general period include projectile points but no ground stone. (The absence of ground stone leads to the "hunting" tag; plant foods were likely prepared in ways other than grinding.) Many sites from this period may no longer be present; soil erosion since the Pleistocene may have eliminated almost all traces of early occupation.

After about 6000 B.C., milling stones and manos become common; projectile points are less frequent and more crudely made. These changes presumably show a shift in diet toward wild plant foods. In the Gila Bend area, though, sites may be rare from 5000 to 3000 B.C. This may have been a period of drought in the southern California desert (Wallace 1978), as well as in the lower Gila basin.

From 3000 B.C. on, Archaic peoples of this region left behind sites with Pinto Basin or related assemblages. This complex included cobble and thick flake choppers and, more notably, characteristic points with weak shoulders and concave bases. Ground stone was mostly cobble manos and shallow-basined slabs; these are rare on open-desert sites (Irwin-Williams 1979: 38). According to Irwin-Williams (1979: 38), Pinto Basin assemblages "represent groups with a mixed foraging economy adapted to lake-edge, river-valley, and succulent-desert environments." At one site in California, Pinto Basin people built circular structures with post supports and dished-out floors (Irwin-Williams 1979: 38-39).

Sometime after 1000 B.C., finely flaked bifacial tools were added to the existing material culture. Farming of a cursory sort might have been adopted in the same period (maize arrived in the Southwest at about this time), but so far there is no evidence to support or deny this.

Ceramic Period

The first people for whom there is direct evidence at Painted Rock are the Hohokam. In the Pioneer period, Hohokam villages are absent from the reservoir area, but they are found in the Sand Tank Mountains nearby (Teague 1981). After A.D. 500, settlement shifted to the Gila River, where irrigation was possible. The Gila Bend area was also a natural crossroads for the growing trade between the middle Gila, the northern Sonora coast (Hayden 1972), and the lower Colorado River (Schroeder 1979: 100, Fig. 1). Colonial period (A.D. 500 to 900) sites in the area included at least one ballcourt (at AZ T:13:9) and the beginnings of another (at AZ Z:2:1) (Wasley and Johnson 1965).

Between A.D. 900 and 1150 (the Sedentary period), Hohokam occupation of the area reached its peak. Extensive canal networks suggest a heavier reliance on farming. The labor invested in those canals, and in the several ballcourts and platform mounds built at AZ Z:2:1 (Wasley and Johnson 1965, Wasley 1960), points to a well-organized society. At the end of the period, however, the irrigation canals and many sites (along with their ballcourts) were abandoned.

Most Classic period (A.D. 1150 to 1450) sites are on or near the floodplain, which suggests farming of seasonally flooded areas. One site, however, is a fortified hilltop (Greenleaf 1975). Schroeder (1961) believes that in the Classic period the Hohokam were replaced by Yuman-speaking peoples; Wasley and Johnson (1965) believe, however, that this was a period of joint occupation.

Historic Period

Nothing is known about human use of the area from A.D. 1450 to 1694, when European explorers found Yuman-speaking villagers along the lower Gila River. These people, ancestral Maricopa, lived by gathering wild plant foods (especially mesquite pods), by floodwater farming, and by hunting and fishing. Their major village was at Gila Bend, the jumping-off point for the trail to the Pima villages. Other Maricopa settlements were scattered to the west and north along the Gila. The Maricopa were constantly fighting the people along the lower Colorado River; by 1850 they were forced to abandon the area, moving eastward (Spier 1933).

After 1700, part of the main land route from northern New Spain to California followed the Gila River. By the 1840s, Anglo-American trappers had passed through the Gila Bend area; one reportedly had a home in the vicinity (Spier 1933: 45). The land north of the Gila was taken by the United States in 1848, and the portion to the south was obtained in 1853. A stage line passed through Gila Bend after 1853 (Berge 1968), and the railroad arrived in 1880. A village of Piman-speakers was founded at the bend of the river prior to 1882, but the area's history was subsequently dominated by Anglo-controlled ranching, prospecting, and irrigation farming.

Chapter 3

SURVEY METHODS

The purpose of the survey was to record and study rock alignment
sites within a 640-acre area and to assess the effects of inundation on
those sites. Any other sites found were also to be recorded and
studied. The methods used in the field are described below.

Study of Aerial Photographs

Before going into the field, we identified a number of possible
features from aerial photos. Most of these showed up on a large-scale
(1:350), vertical, black-and-white photo of most of AZ T:13:22, or "Rock
City," before it was flooded. Given the sparse original plant cover,
even the smallest alignments often could be seen. A Corps of Engineers
study of similar photographs netted a few additional features from the
first photograph that were not originally noted.

High altitude, vertical, color prints (1:12,500) of the
reservoir area were also available. Visible on these were a few
features at AZ T:13:22, alignments at some other sites, and a number of
trails, either aboriginal or bovine (see Other Trails, Chapter 4). Most
identifications were tentative, however, and many features could not be
seen at this scale.

Finally, several low-level, oblique, black-and-white photos and
post-flooding, low-level, vertical, color photos of the area were
checked. These yielded little additional information.

Limits of Survey

Fortunately, it was fairly easy to establish the limits of the
study area. Local topography and vegetation permitted easy location on
USGS quads in most instances. Also, the study area was a single, large,
continuous unit. Actual survey usually went slightly beyond these
limits, however, to make sure that no major sites lurked just over the
line.

AZ T:13:30 (PRS-78-22) and AZ T:13:31 (PRS-78-23)--two sites
listed by the Corps for study--actually lay outside the defined study
area. We recorded these but did not survey the surrounding terrain.

Intensity of Coverage

Two parts of the study area were not surveyed intensively: the old labor camp and the irrigated fields. Both areas were prepared by grading, and the old land surfaces had been destroyed. Because brief visits confirmed the lack of early remains, we did not study these places further.

The remainder of the area was divided into arbitrary units, using features such as jeep trails or the flood line as limits. Each unit was then fully covered by a number of transects. Distance between crew members was about 20 m, with each crew member zigzagging as needed to check the area traversed.

Site Definition and Records

The original intent of the survey was to record all sites on standard Arizona State Museum (ASM) forms (see Appendix B) and to map them with either a transit or plane table and alidade. However, as the nature of the remains became clear, the definition of "site" itself became a problem.

The first consideration is "significance." Remains less than 50 years old do not qualify for National Register status, and usually are not considered significant. During fieldwork such recent materials are normally ignored, and only older materials are considered "sites." In this case, however, the process was not so automatic. It became clear that mixed with the aboriginal rock alignments were others built within the last 50 years. These included some obviously Anglo items, such as hearth rings, but also a number of linear arrangements of rocks resembling the aboriginal ones.

The question was: which alignments were old and which were not? Because in many cases we could not tell, we decided to record all rock features (whether clearly ancient, of unknown age, or clearly recent). We reasoned that the ancient features could later be contrasted with the recent ones, and the resulting criteria for antiquity could then be applied to ambiguous cases. This effort will be discussed further in Chapter 5. It should also be noted that since such features were recorded for comparison rather than as potentially significant remains, the records kept on them were limited.

As a further field concession, the definition of site (those finds rating a full form and plane table map) was restricted to finds with multiple features or artifact concentrations. Many small, simple alignments or clusters of rock were superficial and were not associated with other features or artifacts. In such cases, a short form (Appendix B) was used instead, and scaled drawings (based on tape measurements of key dimensions) were made. (Isolated artifacts were recorded on short forms but not mapped.) No information is lost in these economies of labor, and they allowed us to record 82 finds instead of the estimated 15.

Several large sites or site clusters (AZ T:13:22, the AZ T:13:24 and 25 site cluster, and the AZ T:13:30 and 31 site cluster) were mapped by a Vea Ltd. crew. The surveyors shot in key points, and the ASM crew recorded cultural data (including scaled drawings of each alignment). The cultural data were later combined with the survey plots to produce Map 1 (in pocket). The ASM crew then used a plane table and alidade to map in the remaining sites warranting such treatment, namely: AZ T:13:23, 26, 27, and 28.

Photographs (both black-and-white, and color) were taken of sites and of individual alignments. Exceptions included isolated remains (except alignments), some clearly recent features, and a few features where heavy plant cover made photos impossible. Finally, all sites and isolated finds were plotted on USGS quads.

Sites were given field numbers with the prefix "PRI-". This should not be confused with the prefix used during the 1978 survey, "PRS-78-".

Collections

Only a few sherds were collected in the survey area (Appendix D). In each case, one or two sherds were taken from each site or pottery concentration. Since the concentrations found were from individual pot breaks, these "grab samples" are representative of remaining sherds in each cluster.

Chapter 4

SURVEY RESULTS

In the previous section, survey coverage was discussed. This
chapter describes the cultural remains found and notes any disturbance
or inundation damage to those remains. Finds given ASM site numbers are
described first. Other finds are then described in their order of
discovery.

Throughout the flooded area (below 648 feet), some soil
disturbance has occurred; the coarse particles that once surfaced the
area have been stripped off and reformed into highly localized deposits.
In addition, the basalt rocks which cover so much of the area have lost
their normal dark color and are now pale gray or white. These changes
are assumed in the descriptions that follow, for all sites below the
648-foot level. As stated previously, because comparisons before and
after inundation were rarely possible, statements about inundation
effects at particular locations are somewhat arbitrary.

Judging from surface inspection, almost all remains are
superficial (see Table 6.1, Chapter 6). Site location data are
presented in Appendix A.

Site Descriptions

AZ T:13:22 (PRS-78-16; PRI-1; "Rock City")

First recorded by Teague and Baldwin (1978: 33), AZ T:13:22
consists of a 340-m-by-320-m area containing 43 rock alignment features,
many of them connected by a network of trails (Map 1). Although no
prehistoric artifacts were seen during the pre-inundation survey, many
concentrations of lithic artifacts, and a single potsherd, were found
during this study. The entire area also contains a light scatter of
recent historic trash, most of it from an abandoned labor camp directly
southeast of the site. Low rises within the site have a malpais cover,
while the drainages between tend to have a silty, fairly rock-free
substrate. Site elevation ranges from about 600 feet to 620 feet. The
entire site has been inundated; the original creosote bush community has
been destroyed and replaced with a nearly pure stand of salt cedar.

13

Features

In the following section, rock features are described in the order in which they were found and numbered in the field. Because a few rock aggregates given feature numbers were later found to be natural, the sequence of numbers is broken in some places. In a few cases, two features were erroneously assigned the same number. When such errors were discovered, the two features were distinguished by adding the letters "A" and "B" to the duplicate numbers.

Feature 1

This was found at the southern end of the site. The "feature" (Fig. 4.1) consists of five northwest-southeast trending, straight, multi-coursed rock alignments within a 20-m-by-30-m area. The alignments are from 5 m to 20 m long, and are composed of basalt cobbles. The areas between the alignments are relatively free of gravel and cobbles, in contrast to the malpais cover just outside the feature. The form of the alignments, the cleared areas between them, and the presence of heavy crushing on some of the cobbles all show that the alignments were created by a bulldozer. We start with this feature as a cautionary note that not all rock alignments are aboriginal.

Within and just east of the easternmost alignment, six flakes and one core were found within a 2-m-diameter area. All are of the local, coarse-textured basalt and may be from a single episode of core reduction. This concentration, and another flake found within the westernmost alignment, is only coincidentally associated with the alignments. No inundation damage was noted.

Feature 2

A multi-coursed rock ring was found about 40 m west of Feature 1. In plan view (Fig. 4.2) it is a circle, about 3 m in outside diameter, made of basalt cobbles piled to a height of about 50 cm. The cobble wall is from 60 cm to 80 cm wide, and the interior diameter is about 1.5 m. The interior of the feature is free of cobbles and is slightly dish-shaped. The feature is open to the east, with the "entry" about 1 m wide.

No artifacts, other than a soft drink bottle, were found at Feature 2. The feature interior is crisscrossed with mud cracks, which may have damaged any occupation surface. Otherwise, no disturbance was evident.

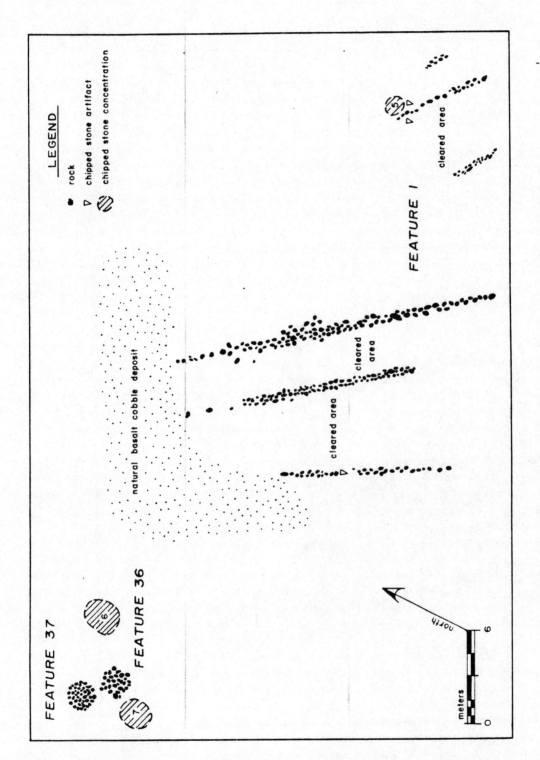

Figure 4.1   AZ T:13:22, Features 1, 36, and 37.

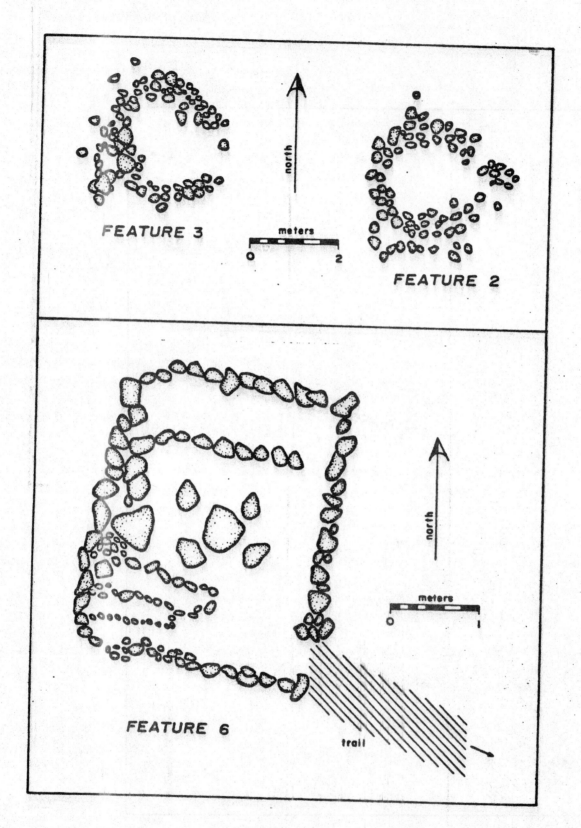

Figure 4.2.   AZ T:13:22, Features 2, 3, and 6.

Feature 3

This feature (Fig. 4.2) is about 4 m west of Feature 2 and is nearly identical to it, the only difference being that the opening in Feature 3 is oriented slightly more to the south. No artifacts were found at Feature 3. Again, the feature interior contains a number of mud cracks; otherwise we did not note any damage.

Feature 4

A multi-coursed rock ring similar to Features 2 and 3, this feature (Fig. 4.3) has an outside diameter of 3 m and an inside diameter of 1.5 m. It is made of basalt cobbles piled to a height of 20 cm to 30 cm. A 1-m-wide break in the wall faces to the east. No artifacts were found at Feature 4, and no disturbance was noted.

Feature 5

This is a D-shaped rock alignment (Fig. 4.3) located about 5 m north of Feature 4. The alignment measures 2.5 m north-south by 2.7 m east-west, and is made of basalt cobbles set one high (10 cm to 30 cm), and one to five wide. In the southwest corner of the feature, a 75-cm-wide opening is present. Compared to the area around it, the inside of the feature is fairly free of gravel and cobbles.

Between Features 4 and 5, two flakes and a core were found within a 2-m-by-3-m area. A concentration of chipped stone (about 30 pieces within a 1-m-diameter area) was found 9 m east-northeast of Feature 5. A similar concentration, with about 30 artifacts within a 2-m-diameter area, was found 10 m north-northwest of Feature 5. All of these artifacts are of the local coarse-textured basalt, and each concentration is probably due to a single episode of core reduction.

No obvious disturbance to Feature 5 could be seen.

Feature 6

This feature is a rectangular stone alignment measuring 3 m north-south by 2.5 m east-west. The interior contains additional alignments. The exterior, rectangular "wall" of the feature is a single course of basalt cobbles (most of them 20 cm to 30 cm in diameter), arranged only one wide in most places. There is a 50-cm opening in the east wall, near the southeast corner (Fig. 4.2).

The northern quarter of the feature interior is partitioned by an east-west alignment; this extends from the west wall to within 30 cm of the east wall. Construction of the internal alignment resembles that of the external wall.

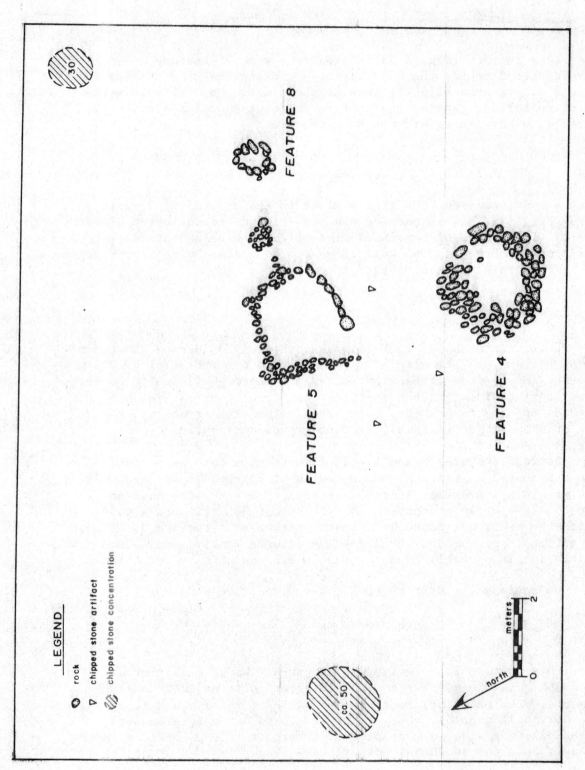

Figure 4.3.   AZ T:13:22, Features 4, 5, and 8.

At the center of the feature there is a large, flat-topped basalt rock, about 50 cm across, around which four smaller (30-cm-diameter) cobbles are equally spaced.

The southwestern corner of the feature is partitioned by three east-west cobble alignments, which extend from the west wall of the feature halfway to the east wall. These alignments are joined at their eastern ends and define two elongate enclosed spaces. The cobbles in these alignments are noticeably smaller (5 cm to 10 cm) than those of the external or northern internal alignments.

No prehistoric artifacts were found at Feature 6. A tapered, chromed steel object (about 10 cm long; possibly part of a hand meat grinder) was found within 3 m of the feature.

No damage from inundation was noted at Feature 6.

Feature 8

A small (1-m-diameter), closed rock ring (Fig. 4.3) was found about 4 m east of Feature 5. The ring is made of basalt cobbles up to 20 cm in diameter, piled one or two high and one wide. No prehistoric artifacts were found in Feature 8, though two lithic artifact concentrations and three other lithic artifacts in the vicinity of Features 4, 5, and 8 have already been noted. No obvious disturbance was seen.

Feature 10

This is a single-coursed, rectangular, basalt-cobble alignment (Fig. 4.4) that measures 2.5 m long by 2.0 m wide, and whose long axis is oriented northwest-southeast. At its north, east, and south corners, there are rectangular alcoves that measure from a maximum of 70 cm by 70 cm (at the southern corner) to a minimum of 50 cm by 50 cm (at the eastern corner). Most cobbles throughout the feature are 10 cm to 20 cm in diameter, though some as large as 40 cm are present.

Just north of the northern corner of the feature is a trail segment marked by a 2.5-m-long, northeast-southwest oriented rock alignment. The alignment is composed of a single line of basalt cobbles, most of them 20 cm to 30 cm in diameter.

No artifacts, prehistoric or historic, were found in or near the feature, which appears to be undisturbed.

Feature 11

Located about 5 m east-northeast of Feature 10, this feature (Fig. 4.4) consists of several single-coursed alignments. A pair of

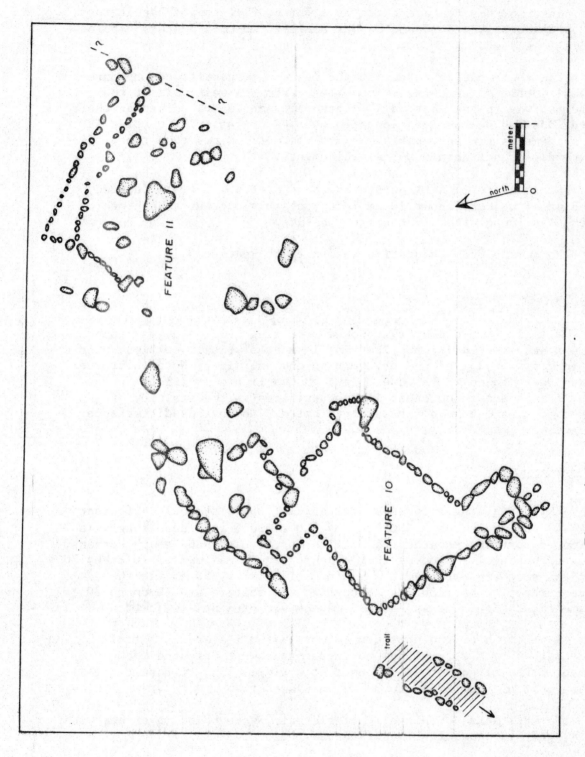

Figure 4.4.   AZ T:13:22, Features 10 and 11.

parallel, northwest-southeast oriented alignments, 2.8 m long and 40 cm apart, are joined at their northwestern ends by a third alignment at right angles to them. The third alignment is 1.5 m long. The feature is made of basalt cobbles 10 cm to 20 cm in diameter.

No artifacts were found in association with this feature, and no disturbance of the feature was noted.

Feature 13

This is a partial rock ring measuring 1.6 m north-south by 1.3 m east-west (Fig. 4.5). It includes a large (60-cm-diameter) rock, around which smaller basalt cobbles (20 cm to 40 cm in diameter) have been piled from one to three high to form an irregular crescent opening to the east.

No artifacts were found at the feature, nor was any inundation damage noticed.

Feature 14

A small rectangular rock alignment (Fig. 4.5), this feature measures 1.2 m east-west by 90 cm north-south. The feature consists of a single line of about 15 basalt cobbles, which are from 10 cm to 30 cm in diameter.

No artifacts were found, nor was any inundation damage seen.

Feature 15

Feature 15 (Fig. 4.5) is a small, oval rock ring measuring 1 m east-west by 80 cm north-south. It is made of about 15 basalt cobbles from 10 cm to 30 cm in diameter, piled one to two high. No artifacts were found in association with Feature 15, and inundation has had no observable effect on the feature.

Feature 16

This is an oval ring of basalt cobbles (Fig. 4.5) very similar to Feature 15, except that it is slightly smaller (80 cm east-west by 60 cm north-south). As was the case at Feature 15, no artifacts or inundation damage were seen.

Feature 17A

This feature (Fig. 4.6) is a single-coursed, rectangular rock alignment with its long axis oriented northwest-southeast. The

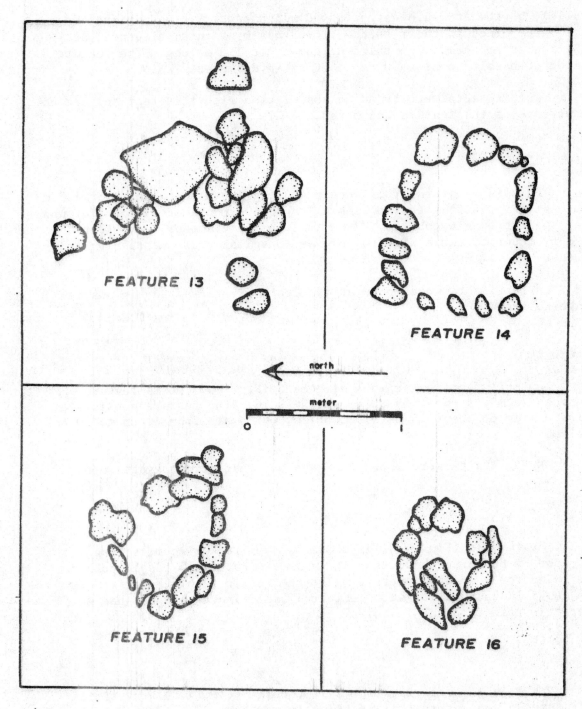

FEATURE 13

FEATURE 14

north

meter

0

FEATURE 15

FEATURE 16

Figure 4.5.   AZ T:12:22, Features 13, 14, 15, and 16.

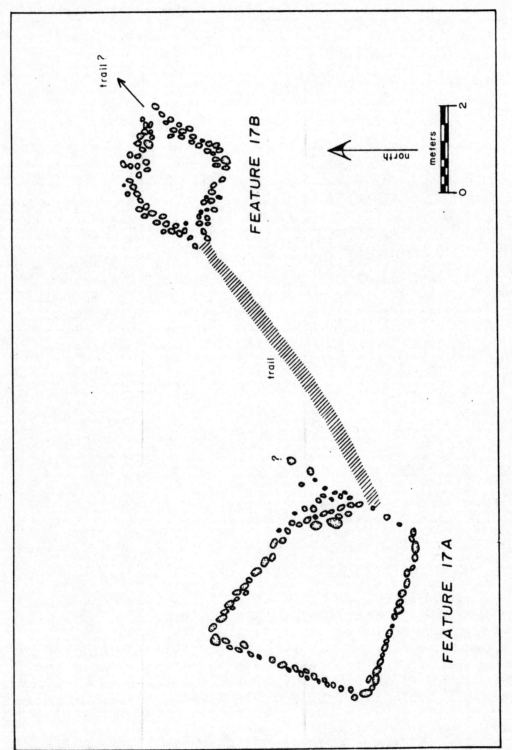

Figure 4.6.   AZ T:13:22, Features 17A and 17B.

northwest, northeast, southeast, and southwest sides of the rectangle are 4.0 m, 4.4 m, 3.0 m, and 3.8 m long, respectively. The basalt cobbles that make up the alignment are from 10 cm to 30 cm in diameter. With the exception of a small (1-m-by-1-m) cobble concentration at the east corner, the interior of the feature is clear of cobbles.

A trail, leading northeast to Feature 17B, begins at the southeastern side of Feature 17A.

No artifacts were found in or near Feature 17A, and inundation has had no obvious effect on it.

Feature 17B

This multi-coursed rock ring (Fig. 4.6) measures 2.4 m in outside diameter and has an inside diameter of 1.8 m. The ring is made of basalt cobbles up to 30 cm in diameter, piled one to two high, and two to four wide. Compared to the surrounding area, the interior is relatively clear of cobbles.

A northeast-southwest oriented trail passes through this rock ring (which, in effect, forms a wide spot in the trail). The openings for the trail are 50 cm wide; in one direction the trail leads to Feature 17A, and in the other direction it eventually ends. No artifacts were found in or near Feature 17B, and inundation resulted in no obvious disturbance to the feature.

Feature 20

A small, single-coursed, rectangular rock alignment (Fig. 4.7), Feature 20 measures 1 m east-west by 70 cm north-south. It is built of about 20 basalt cobbles from 10 cm to 30 cm in diameter.

No artifacts were found with the feature, and inundation apparently has caused little or no damage to it.

Feature 22A

This feature (Fig. 4.8) is a north-south oriented, rectilinear, multi-coursed rock alignment measuring 1.8 m by 0.4 m. It is up to 50 cm high. The feature consists of basalt cobbles up to 30 cm in diameter, piled two high and two wide. A small (50-cm-diameter) cairn made of six cobbles 20 cm to 30 cm in diameter, and a 1-m-long rock alignment composed of a line of four cobbles 30 cm to 40 cm in diameter, are found 6 m northeast of the main feature. These two items, however, could be of natural origin.

No artifacts were associated with Feature 22A, nor was any inundation damage apparent.

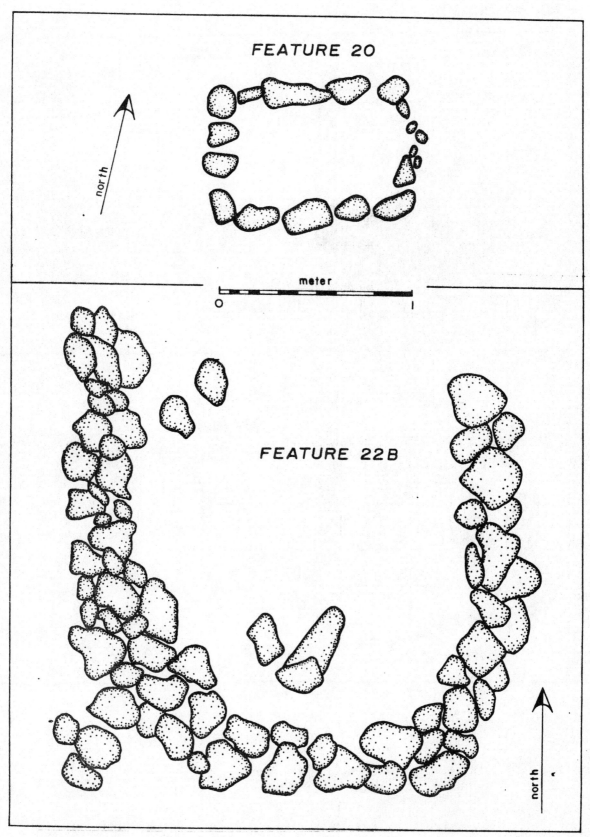

FEATURE 20

north

meter

0   1

FEATURE 22B

north

Figure 4.7.   AZ T:13:22, Features 20 and 22B.

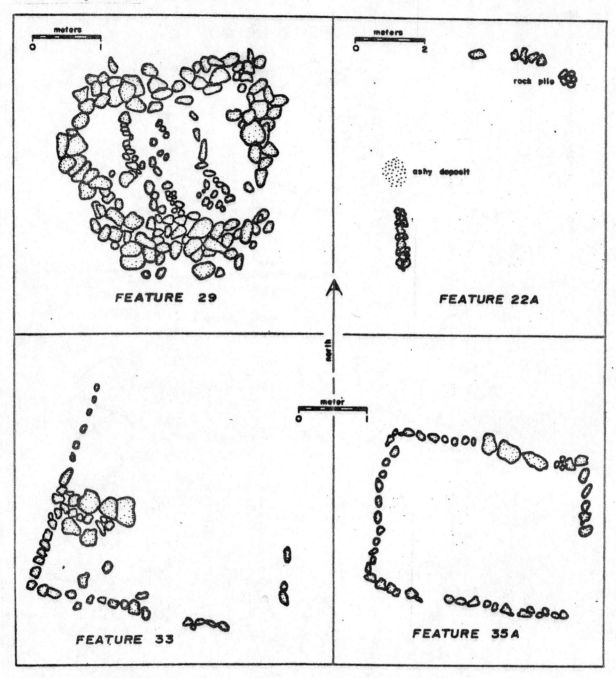

Figure 4.8.   AZ T:12:22, Features 22A, 29, 33, and 35A.

Feature 22B

Feature 22B (Fig. 4.7) is a partial rock ring measuring 2.5 m
east-west by 2.0 m north-south, and consists of cobbles 10 cm to 30 cm
in diameter piled two or three wide and high. A 1.5-m-wide gap in the
wall opens the feature to the north. The area within the feature is
relatively free of cobbles.

No artifacts were found at the feature. Inundation has caused
little, if any, disturbance.

Feature 23

This is a complex, rectilinear, basalt cobble feature whose
internal area is partitioned by a number of alignments (Fig. 4.9). The
maximum extent of the feature is 6.5 m north-south by 8.0 m east-west.
In much of the feature, especially the southern half, the alignments are
composed of a single course of cobbles 10 cm to 30 cm in diameter. In
the northern half of the feature, the alignments tend to be
multi-coursed, consisting of somewhat larger cobbles piled two or three
wide and one or two high. Compared with the area immediately outside
the feature, the interior is relatively clear. A northeast-to-southwest
trail runs along the northeast side of the feature.

The only artifacts associated with Feature 23 are a basalt core
included in one of the alignments, and a piece of wire garden fence, 50
cm by 30 cm, lying inside the feature.

A comparison of a pre-inundation photograph and one taken after
flooding (Figs. 4.10, 4.11) indicates that little movement of rocks
resulted from flooding.

Feature 24

Feature 24 (Fig. 4.12) is a circular rock pile 1.2 m in diameter
and 50 cm high. It contains basalt cobbles that are from 10 cm to 30 cm
in diameter.

Three trails pass within 6 m of the feature. One of these
extends northeast from the rock pile for 5 m, where it joins a second,
north-south oriented trail. At the southwestern corner of the junction
of these two trails, about 10 flakes and flake fragments (all of
coarse-textured basalt, probably struck from the same core) were found
in a 1-m-diameter area. The third trail, also north-south oriented,
passes 6 m west of Feature 24. Three cores and two flakes of
coarse-textured basalt were found in a 2-m-diameter area along the east
side of this trail, about 8 m north-northwest of Feature 24.

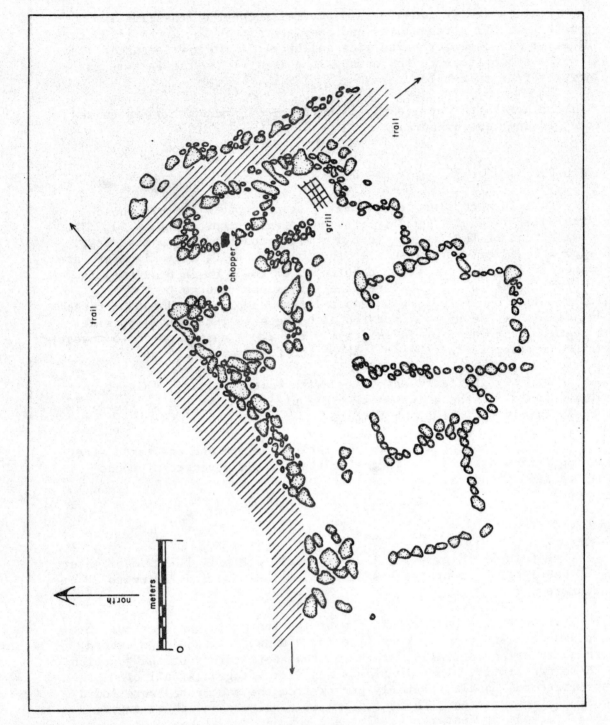

Figure 4.9.   AZ T:13:22, Feature 23.

Figure 4.10. AZ T:13:22, Feature 23 before inundation.

Figure 4.11. AZ T:13:22, Feature 23 after inundation.

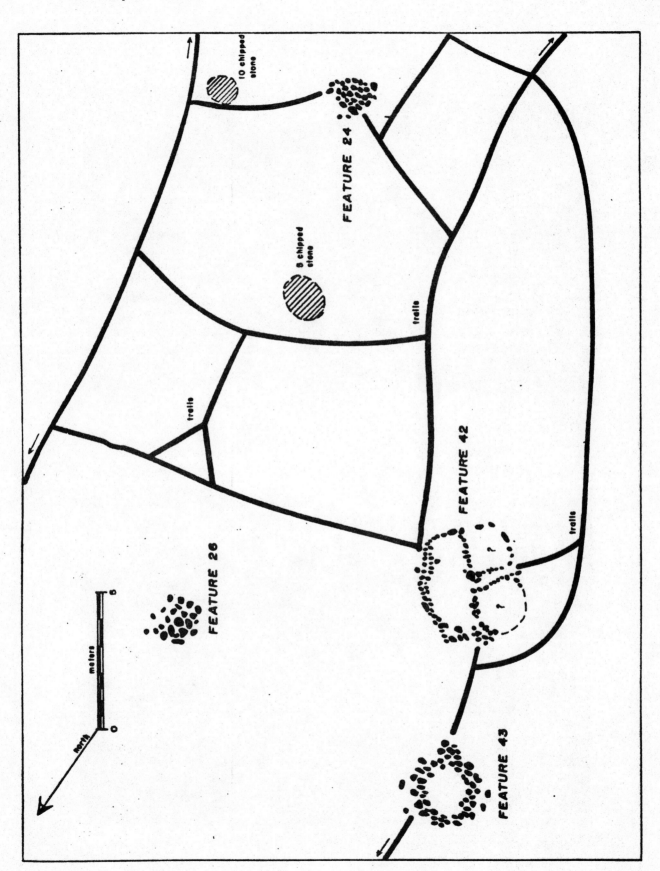

Figure 4.12. AZ T:13:22, Features 24, 26, 42, and 43.

Feature 26

This is a rock pile similar to Feature 24, and is located about 20 m northwest of it. Feature 26 (Fig. 4.12) is about 1.4 m in diameter, about 50 cm high, and is made of basalt cobbles from 10 cm to 40 cm in diameter.

Other than the two concentrations of chipped stone described with Feature 24, no artifacts were found at or near Feature 26.

Inundation has apparently had little or no effect on the feature.

Feature 28A

A small (1.5-m-diameter) rock ring (Fig. 4.13), Feature 28A consists of a single course of small (10-cm diameter) basalt cobbles about 10 cm apart. The interior of the ring is clear, and no artifacts were found.

With the exception of 1 cm to 2 cm of silt deposition, inundation has probably had little or no effect on the feature.

Feature 28B

This feature is a small (1-m-diameter) rock ring (Fig. 4.13) made from a single row of basalt cobbles spaced about 10 cm apart. It is very similar to, but slightly smaller than, Feature 28A, which is only 2 m northeast.

No artifacts were found and, with the exception of the shallow silt deposition just mentioned, inundation has had no obvious effect on this feature.

Feature 29

Feature 29 (Fig. 4.8) is a subrectangular, multi-coursed rock alignment measuring 3 m by 3 m. It is composed of basalt cobbles 10 cm to 30 cm in diameter, piled one to four wide and high. A 50-cm-wide opening is present at the alignment's southeast corner. Within the otherwise cleared interior of the feature, three parallel north-south alignments are present. They break the interior into four separate areas, and are composed of small cobbles 5 cm to 10 cm in diameter arranged one or two wide and only one high. The central and western internal alignments extend from the north to the south exterior walls. The easternmost internal alignment extends from the north wall towards the south wall, but ends in a small (40-cm-diameter) loop before reaching the south wall. No artifacts were found near Feature 29.

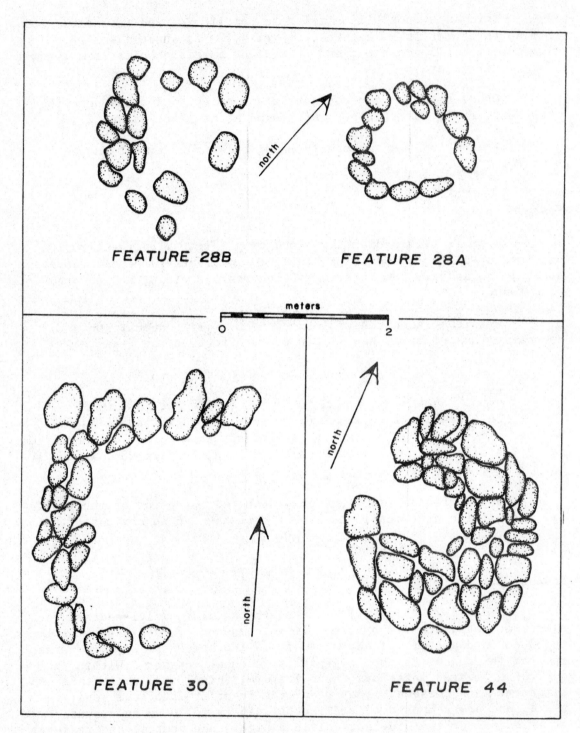

FEATURE 28B   FEATURE 28A

FEATURE 30   FEATURE 44

Figure 4.13. AZ T:13:22, Features 23A, 28B, 30, and 44.

Comparison between a pre-inundation photograph and one taken after flooding (Figs. 4.14, 4.15) shows that relatively minor movement of cobbles has occurred, presumably as a result of inundation. Movement was limited to the smaller cobbles forming the internal alignments. It is more difficult to assess the effect of flooding on caliche deposits, as nearly all cobbles have been either "bleached" or stained to a uniformly light color.

Feature 30

A three-sided, rectilinear rock feature open to the east (Fig. 4.13), Feature 30 is about 5 m west-southwest of Feature 29. The alignment is composed of a single row of cobbles 20 cm to 30 cm in diameter and its north, west, and south sides measure 2.5 m, 3.0 m, and 1.5 m, respectively. No artifacts were found in association with Feature 30, nor was any inundation damage apparent.

Feature 33

This feature is an L-shaped rectilinear alignment (Fig. 4.8), with a west side 3.0 m long and the south side 3.5 m long. A few cobbles possibly represent an east side to the alignment. From the approximate midpoint of the west side, another possible alignment extends toward the interior of the feature for about 1.3 m. The external alignments are made from cobbles 10 cm to 20 cm in diameter arranged in single rows, while the internal "alignment" contains rocks up to 40 cm in diameter, arranged one high and up to three wide.

No artifacts were found at Feature 33, and with the exception of shallow silt deposition, no disturbance was apparent.

Feature 34

A multi-coursed, J-shaped enclosure opening to the west (Fig. 4.16), Feature 34 measures 5 m by 2.5 m. The north wall is 3 m long, and more or less straight. At the east end of the north side, the alignment turns sharply south, and continues for 3 m before curving sharply back (thus forming the east, south, and west sides of the feature). The alignment continues northward before ending 1 m south of the north wall. The alignment is made of basalt cobbles 10 cm to 40 cm in diameter piled up to three high and five wide. The alignment is 50 cm high and 1 m wide, but was probably higher in the past.

Three trails were noted at Feature 34. One extends southeast from the southern tip of the enclosure. Another trail, oriented north-south, passes next to the west end of the north wall and the "entrance." This trail is marked along its west side by a 2-m-long,

Figure 4.14.   AZ T:13:22, Feature 29 before inundation.

Figure 4.15.   AZ T:13:22, Feature 29 after inundation.

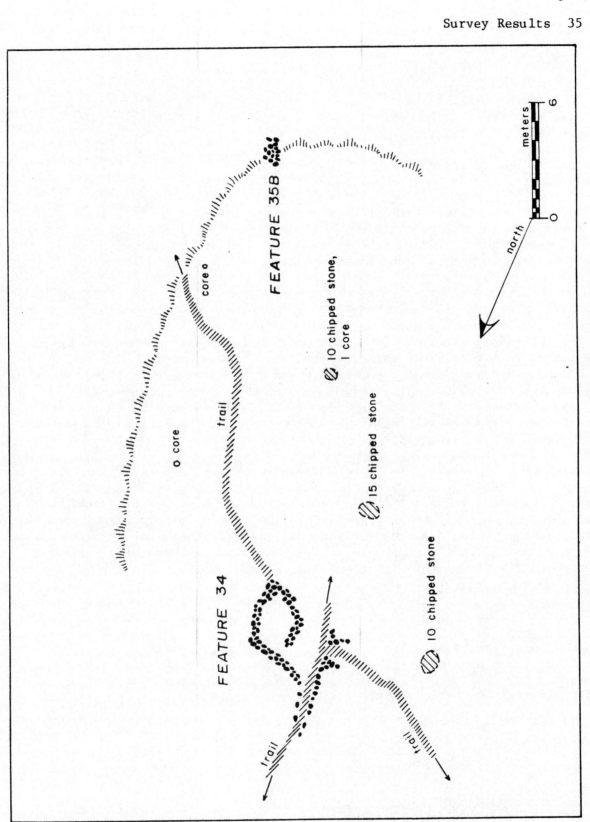

core o

O core

trail

FEATURE 35B

FEATURE 34

10 chipped stone,
1 core

15 chipped stone

10 chipped stone

trail

trail

north

meters

0   6

Figure 4.16. AZ T:13:22, Features 34 and 35B.

50-cm-high, multi-coursed, basalt cobble alignment. Just south of this alignment, the third trail extends to the northeast.

About 10 lithic artifacts, all of local basalt, were found in a 2-m-diameter area, 8.5 m west of the center of the enclosure. A similar concentration, containing about 15 artifacts, was found 7.5 m south-southwest of the center of the enclosure. Each of these artifact concentrations is probably due to reduction of a single core. An isolated core was found 10 m southeast of the feature.

In the cleared interior of the feature, several small pieces of charcoal were found. We could not tell whether these are associated with the structure, or whether they floated in during flooding. Otherwise, no inundation effects were noted.

Feature 35A

This is a single-coursed, rectangular cobble alignment, 3 m long and 2 m wide (Fig. 4.8). It is located 5 m north of Feature 33. There is a 1-m-wide opening in the southeast corner, along the east side. Most of the cobbles are 10 cm to 20 cm in diameter; three adjacent cobbles on the north side are 30 cm to 40 cm in diameter. No artifacts were found, and minor silting was the only apparent inundation effect.

Feature 35B

This is a 50-cm-diameter, 30-cm-high pile of six basalt cobbles, each about 20 cm in diameter (Fig. 4.16). About nine basalt flakes and one core were found in a 1-m-diameter area, 12 m southeast of Feature 35B; core was found 7 m northwest of the feature. No inundation damage was apparent.

Feature 36

This feature is a 2-m-diameter, 20-cm-high, circular pile of basalt cobbles, most of which are 10 cm to 20 cm in diameter (Fig. 4.1). About six basalt flakes were found in a 2-m-diameter area, 3 m east of this feature. No obvious inundation damage was seen.

Feature 37

Feature 37 (Fig. 4.1) is a circular pile of basalt cobbles nearly identical to Feature 36, which is 1 m to the south. No artifacts, other than the flakes east of Feature 36, were found near Feature 37. No inundation damage was apparent.

Feature 38

This is a single-coursed, rectangular, basalt cobble alignment measuring 3.5 m north-south by 3.0 m east-west (Fig. 4.17). An alignment, beginning on the east side 80 cm north of the southeast corner, extends 1.8 m across the feature interior. There is a 75-cm gap in the south side of the feature and a 50-cm gap in the west side; both are near the southwest corner. Most of the cobbles are 20 cm to 30 cm in diameter, though the northwest corner is made of smaller ones 5 cm to 10 cm in diameter. No inundation damage was noted, nor were any artifacts found.

Feature 39

This feature is a 4-m-diameter, 50-cm-high, multi-coursed rock ring, opening to the northwest (Fig. 4.17). The interior is partly filled in with cobbles. Most of the cobbles from which the ring was made are 20 cm to 40 cm in diameter. A 1.5-m-wide cleared area surrounds the southern half of the ring. A trail extends from this area to the southeast. No artifacts were found.

Feature 39 is on a moderate slope and was subjected to wave action that seems to have partly undermined the ring. In the pre-inundation, low-level, black-and-white aerial photo of AZ T:13:22, the ring wall, opening, and interior appear more distinct than during the recent survey. This suggests that inundation caused some damage to the feature.

Feature 40

A single-coursed, irregular-oval, closed rock alignment (Fig. 4.18), Feature 40 is made of cobbles 10 cm to 20 cm in diameter. The enclosure's maximum dimensions are 2 m (north-south) by 1.4 m (east-west). A well-defined trail, marked by parallel, discontinuous rows of cobbles, extends east from the northeast corner of the enclosure for a distance of at least 7 m. The trail is about 40 cm wide.

A large (40-cm-diameter) basalt cobble with one lightly ground surface was found 7 m northeast of the enclosure. This is the only piece of ground stone found during the survey. No other artifacts were seen, and no inundation damage was noted.

Feature 41

This is an L-shaped rock alignment (Fig. 4.17) 2 m long and 1.4 m wide. It is made of cobbles 10 to 20 cm in diameter arranged discontinuously in single rows. Although a few cobbles outside the alignment suggest a closed rectangle, the low-level, pre-inundation

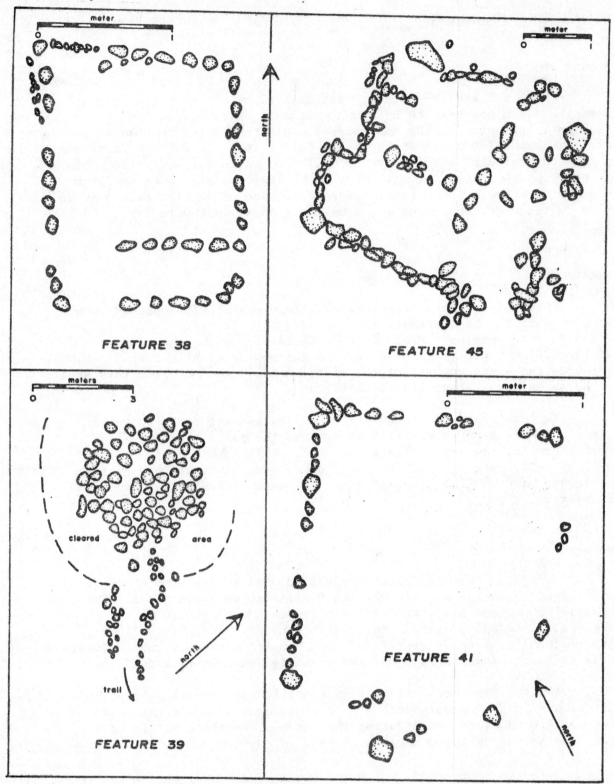

Figure 4.17.   AZ T:13:22, Features 38, 39, 41, and 45.

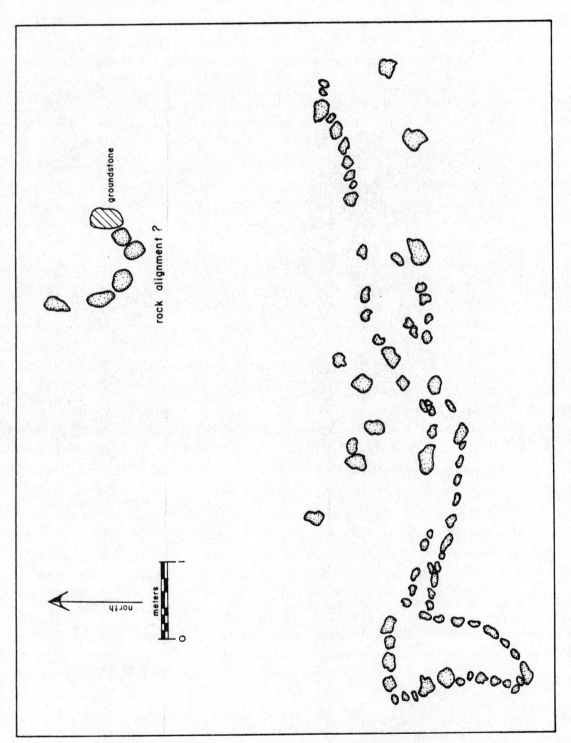

groundstone

rock alignment ?

north

meters

Figure 4.18. AZ T:13:22, Feature 40.

aerial photo of AZ T:13:22 shows that flooding has not changed the configuration of the feature. No artifacts were found.

Feature 42

This feature (Fig. 4.12) is an elongate rock enclosure, 2 m by 4 m in size, with its long axis roughly east-west. In plan view, the eastern portion of the enclosure consists of a 2-m-diameter circular alignment joined to, but not partitioned from, a 2-m-by-2-m-diameter sub-rectangular alignment (which forms the western portion of the feature). The walls are made of cobbles 10 cm to 30 cm in diameter piled one or two high and wide. A well-defined trail, marked by two parallel rows of cobbles, extends southward from the south "wall" of the enclosure; trail width is about 50 cm. The feature interior is clear, as are two other, 2-m-diameter areas on either side of the trail, just south of the enclosure.

Comparison of pre- and post-inundation photographs (Figs. 4.19, 4.20) shows little, if any, disturbance from inundation. No artifacts were found with Feature 42.

Feature 43

This is a multi-coursed rock ring (Fig. 4.12) similar to Features 2 and 3. The ring has an external diameter of 2.5 m, and its cleared interior is 1.5 m in diameter. The "wall" is about 50 cm tall, and is made with 10-cm- to 40-cm-diameter basalt cobbles piled two or three high and wide. An opening in the alignment faces northwest. No artifacts or disturbance to the feature were seen.

Feature 44

This feature is a 1.5-m-diameter, 30-cm-high, rock ring that opens to the west (Figure 4.13). The ring is made of cobbles 20 cm to 30 cm in diameter piled two or three high and wide. A few cobbles in the 1-m-diameter interior may have fallen in from the walls, suggesting that the walls may have been higher at one time. Pre-inundation photographs show a trail leading up to the "entrance" of the ring from the southwest, and then bending sharply away to the northwest. These were erased by inundation. However, comparison of pre- and post-inundation photos (Figs. 4.21, 4.22) also suggests that little disturbance of the ring itself has occurred. No artifacts were found.

Feature 45

This feature (Fig. 4.17) is a 3-m-by-3-m square rock alignment made of basalt cobbles 10 cm to 40 cm in diameter set one or two wide

Figure 4.19. AZ T:13:22, Feature 42 before inundation.

Figure 4.20. AZ T:13:22, Feature 42 after inundation.

Figure 4.21. AZ T:13:22, Feature 44 before inundation.

Figure 4.22. AZ T:13:22, Feature 44 after inundation.

and one high. A T-shaped internal alignment defines three areas within
the feature, one in the northwest (2 m by 1.5 m), one in the southwest
(2 m by 1.3 m), and one in the east (3 m by 1 m). Both the northeast
and southeast corners are open. No artifacts were seen, and with the
exception of small mudcracks in the surface on which the alignment was
located, no inundation damage was noted.

Feature 46

This is a multi-coursed, northeast-southwest oriented, oval rock
enclosure, 2 m long and 1.5 m wide (Figure 4.23). It is made of basalt
cobbles 10 cm to 15 cm in diameter piled two or three high and wide.
The southeastern end of the oval is open, and the northeastern third of
the cleared interior is closed off by an internal alignment made of
several larger cobbles 30 cm to 40 cm in diameter. No artifacts were
found, and inundation has apparently not disturbed the feature.

Feature 47

This is a J-shaped, multi-coursed rock enclosure measuring 5.5 m
(east-west) by 4.0 m (north-south) (Fig. 4.23). The enclosure walls are
30 cm to 1 m wide and are made of basalt cobbles 10 cm to 40 cm in
diameter piled one or two high. The northwest portion of the alignment
consists of a fairly orderly double row of stones. There are two
50-cm-wide openings in the alignment, one in the north and one in the
southeast. A 1-m-long by 50-cm-wide, irregular cobble pile is located
1 m southeast of the southeastern corner of the enclosure. About eight
lithic artifacts, all of local basalt, were found in a 1-m-diameter
area, 15 m south of the feature; a single flake of basalt was found 10 m
east of the enclosure. Inundation has had no apparent effect on the
feature (Figs. 4.24 and 4.25).

Feature 48

This feature (Fig. 4.23) is a 40-cm-diameter, 15-cm-high,
circular pile of cobbles 5 cm to 10 cm in diameter piled one to three
high. No artifacts or inundation disturbance were noted.

Feature 50

Feature 50 (Fig. 4.23) is a D-shaped rock alignment measuring
2.4 m (north-south) by 2.6 m (east-west). The alignment is composed of
cobbles 10 cm to 30 cm in diameter arranged one or two wide and one
high. There is a 60-cm-wide opening in the northeast corner. Along a
trail extending east from the feature, five basalt flakes and the core
from which they were struck were found in a 2-m-diameter area, 20 m east
of the enclosure. No inundation damage was apparent (Figs. 4.26 and
4.27).

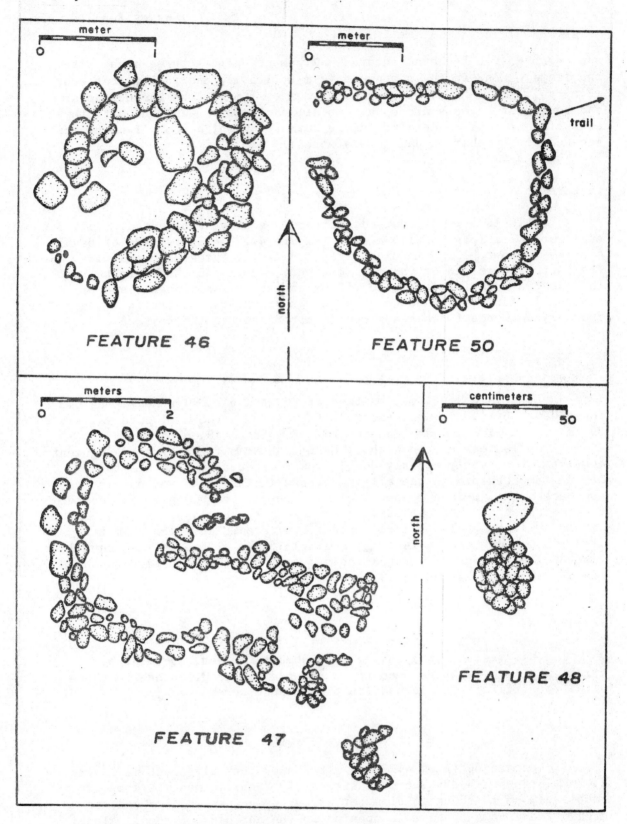

Figure 4.23.   AZ T:13:22, Features 46, 47, 48 and 50.

Figure 4.24. AZ T:13:22, Feature 47 before inundation.

Figure 4.25. AZ T:13:22, Feature 47 after inundation.

Figure 4.26.   AZ T:13:22, Feature 50 before inundation.

Figure 4.27.   AZ T:13:22, Feature 50 after inundation.

Trails

About 430 m of trail segments were found within the site during the survey. Most of these are cleared areas 40 cm to 1.5 m wide bordered by single rows of cobbles. These rows of cobbles extend from the features for up to 60 m before encountering other features or disappearing.

On a pre-inundation aerial photo, a much more extensive network of trails is visible--at least 1200 m, counting those segments found on the ground during survey. It is thus apparent that flooding has had a substantial effect on the integrity of the trail system. In most cases, trail segments found during the survey were on low ridges densely covered with basalt cobbles, and were easily recognized. However, trails in less rocky areas, such as drainages, or marked by less substantial alignments, were more prone to inundation damage. These may have been obscured by shallow silting and dense tamarisk stands, or may simply have been erased by wave action.

Other Artifacts

In addition to those artifacts already described along with features, "isolated" flakes and cores, all of local basalt, were encountered throughout the site. Only one potsherd was found (Map 1); this is a Pioneer Hohokam sherd (A.D. 1 to 500), probably Snaketown Red-on-buff. A very low density of recent trash, including cans, bottle glass, wire, and shotgun shells, was also found throughout the site.

AZ T:13:22:   Concluding Comments

Rock City contains an extensive assortment of trails, rock alignments, and aboriginal artifacts, as well as a thin scatter of recent trash. It appears that at least some alignments were created recently by children from the adjacent abandoned labor camp. The distorting effect of child's play is poorly understood in archaeology (Hammond and Hammond 1981); here it has seriously limited our ability to interpret the remains, making it difficult to say which alignments are aboriginal and which are recent. Still, the site clearly has a substantial aboriginal component that can at least be partly isolated.

AZ T:13:24 (PRI-4)

This site (Fig. 4.28) is on a low knoll which is a terrace remnant at the edge of the Gila floodplain. The natural ground cover is a dense carpet of basalt cobbles. This appears to have been a substantial site, but flooding has damaged it heavily and obscured the original boundaries. Remains now cover a 50-m-by-30-m area. A length

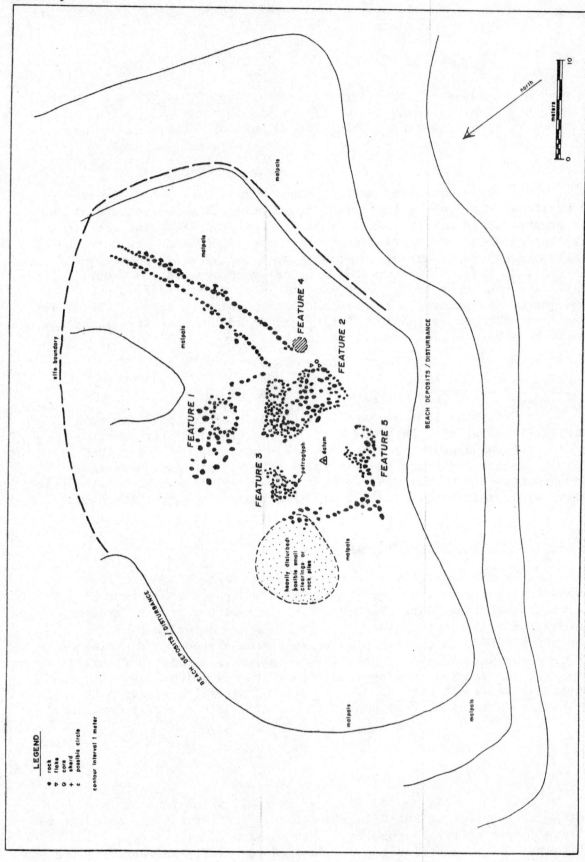

Figure 4.28.   AZ T:13:23.

of 2-inch white PVC pipe was set across the road from this site, to aid relocation.

Description of Remains

Feature 1

This is an oval cleared area, about 2.5 m by 1.5 m, within the malpais cover. Basalt cobbles removed from the cleared area were placed at its perimeter.

Feature 2

This 10-m-by-15-m feature was badly disturbed by flooding. It appears to be a rearrangement of the malpais cover into a cluster of two or three rock circles, which are 75 cm to 1.5 m across. Two cores and two flakes of basalt were found at this feature.

Feature 3

This is another cluster of rocks which appears to contain two or three small circular clearings. The cluster measures 4 m by 3 m, with the clearings about 50 cm to 1.5 m across. In the cluster is a basalt rock, about 30 cm across, with a petroglyph on it (Fig. 4.29). The latter is a small oval connected to a short line curving around it. A basalt flake was found 1.5 m south of the feature.

Feature 4

A cluster of about 20 basalt flakes was found in a 1.5-m-by-1-m area roughly 2 m east of Feature 2.

Feature 5

This rock circle is 1 m in diameter, open to the north. A single sherd of Gila Plain (?) was found inside.

Trail

A trail runs from Feature 2 to the northeast; it becomes indistinct after dropping off the knoll. The trail's width averages about one meter. A second trail, running northwest, appears in an aerial photograph but was not visible on the ground.

Figure 4.29.   AZ T:13:23, petroglyph.

Figure 4.30.   AZ T:13:30, Feature 6, petroglyph.

Other Remains

A cluster of three basalt flakes was noted about 5 m southwest of Feature 3. A few additional pieces of chipped stone are scattered about the site.

Inundation Effects

As mentioned before, inundation is substantial. All features have been disturbed to some degree. Some soil and rock movement has occurred; inferentially, artifact movement has also taken place.

AZ T:13:24 (PRI-6)

Like AZ T:13:23, this site is on the tip of a terrace remnant just out of the Gila floodplain (Fig. 4.31). The ground is covered with a thick layer of basalt cobbles, some of which have been partly reduced, presumably to obtain crude but useful flakes or cores. Clearly, this is a special use site; unlike AZ T:13:23, the ground at this site is too steep to allow habitation.

The site covers about 135 m by 45 m. Several chipping stations are identifiable; in addition, isolated flakes and cores are scattered throughout the malpais cover. To aid in relocation, a length of 2-inch white PVC pipe was set across the road from the site.

Description of Remains

Feature 1

This chipping station contains about 100 cortical and noncortical basalt flakes within a 1.5-m-diameter area. It is probably from a single episode of core reduction.

Feature 2

Here are about 15 basalt flakes, all from the same core (not seen), in a 70-cm-diameter area.

Feature 3

This location includes 2 cores and 5 flakes of basalt in a 1.5-m-diameter area. Two episodes of core reduction are indicated.

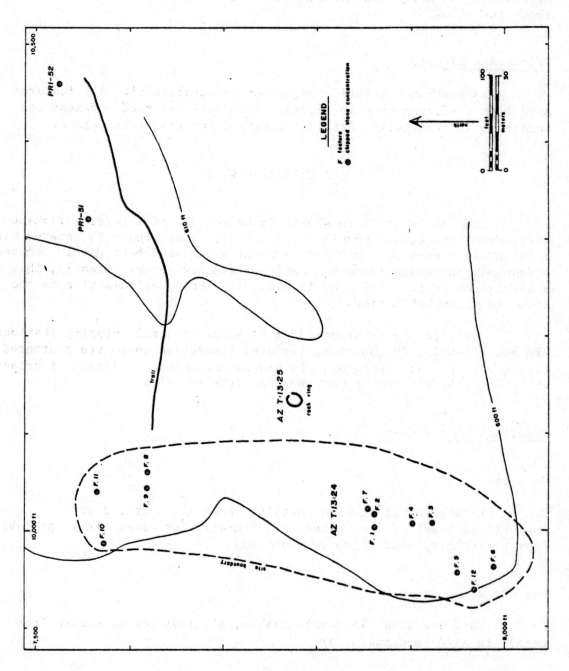

Figure 4.31. AZ T:13:24 and AZ T:13:25; PRI-51 and PRI-52.

Feature 4

At least 10 basalt flakes are present in a 1-m-diameter area.
They are probably from the same core (not seen).

Feature 5

At least 10 basalt flakes (from the same core, not seen) were
found in a 3-m-diameter area. These flakes are very large (up to 20 cm
long); perhaps the missing core was a metate in early stages of
preparation.

Feature 6

A core and at least 9 flakes are present in a 5-m-by-2-m area.
Variation in the basalt used suggests several different episodes of core
reduction. This feature has been somewhat scattered by wave action.

Feature 7

At least 5 flakes of vesicular basalt are present in a
40-m-diameter area. These were struck from the same core (not present).

Feature 8

A large core and about 30 flakes of vesicular basalt were found
in a 3-m-diameter area. Two episodes of reduction are present; the
second core has been removed. The flakes are up to 15 cm long; perhaps
this chipping station represents two attempts (one successful) at
initial preparation of a metate.

Feature 9

This feature includes at least 10 basalt flakes and a
15-cm-diameter basalt cobble core. The core has a few flake scars at
one end; the same end is battered, suggesting use as a hammerstone.

Feature 10

At least 10 flakes and 3 cores, all of basalt, were found in a
2-m-diameter area. The cores are small (5 cm to 10 cm across) cobbles
with unifacial flake removal at one end.

Feature 11

About 15 flakes and 3 cores of basalt were found in a 2-m-diameter area. Most of the flakes are probably from the same core (not found).

Feature 12

A half dozen flakes, some cortical, were found in a 1-m-by-1-m area.

Inundation Effects

Much of the site has been affected by wave action. At least 5 cm of soil has been lost in the hardest hit areas. By inference, some degree of artifact movement has also occurred.

AZ T:13:25 (PRI-9)

This site is located on the same terrace finger as AZ T:13:24, but is farther back from the edge of the floodplain (Fig. 4.31). The malpais cover also occurs here. The site is a rock ring (Fig. 4.32), of the sort often associated with early occupations of the region. The cleared area is 2.5 m in diameter, with the surrounding ring (of basalt cobbles) being one course high, and about 75 cm wide. Careful inspection failed to reveal any caliche on the cobbles; the general impression is of great antiquity. So far, the site has not been significantly disturbed.

About 15 flakes of coarse local basalt were found inside the ring. These may postdate the feature. Also, three cores were found within 10 m of the sleeping circle.

AZ T:13:26 (PRI-12)

This site is located on a point of the bluff that dominates the study area. It is an obvious place to ascend or descend the bluff, and a prehistoric trail apparently passed this way (see Other Trails, this chapter). It is also a good temporary campsite, as it is fairly flat and has a good view of the area (Fig. 4.33).

Site limits are defined by artifacts scattered over a 55-m-by-20-m area. Several episodes of use may be present. Some of the chipped stone is heavily patinated in a way that will have a few archaeologists muttering about a "pre-altithermal" component. We will limit ourselves, however, to the statement that a Preceramic component

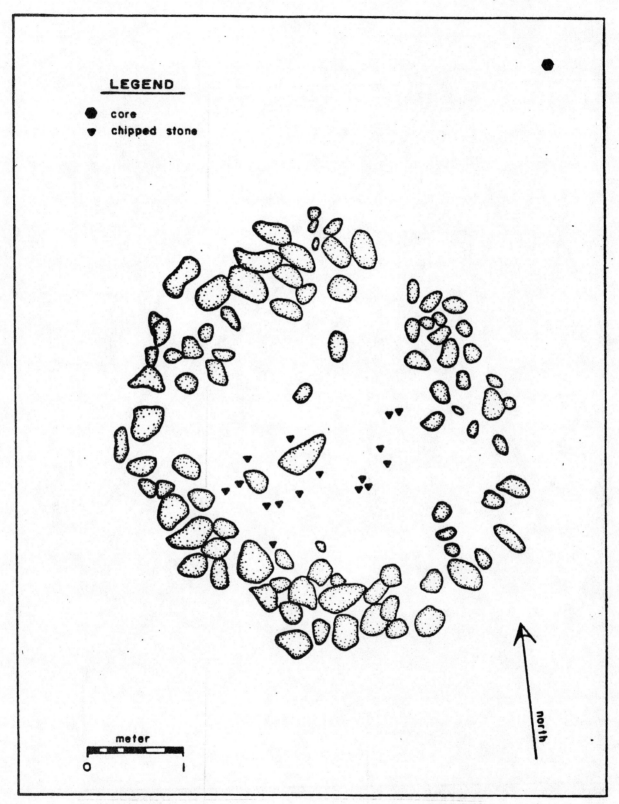

Figure 4.32.   AZ T:13:25, detail map of rock ring.

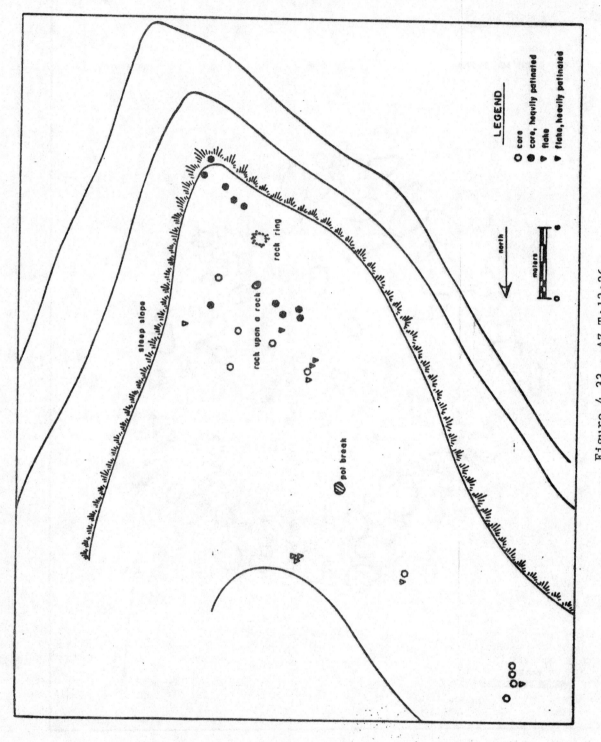

Figure 4.33. AZ T:13:26.

is likely. The other pieces of chipped stone lack this heavy patination and may be much younger. Almost all the chipped stone is basalt; a few pieces of fine-grained nonlocal stone are present.

A rock ring, 1.5 m in diameter and one or two rocks high and wide, is present near the end of the point. Four meters north of it is a rock with another rock on top of it. In addition, sherds from a Sacaton Red-on-buff jar were found in a small cluster north and west of the rock features.

The site, outside the 661-foot inundation zone, is undisturbed.

AZ T:13:27 (PRI-23)

This site is in an area of low, cobble-topped rises that alternate with silty drainages. It consists of two rock alignment features connected by a trail. No artifacts were found. To aid in relocation, a datum of 2-inch white PVC pipe was set at the site (Fig. 4.34). Site extent is 55 m by 15 m.

Feature 1 is a complex rock alignment which straddles a small, silty drainage. Rocks used range from 5 cm to over 30 cm in size, with most being about 10 cm; these were placed one or two wide and one (rarely two) high. A trapezoidal "main room" measures about 7 m by 3 m; it is mostly cleared but contains several large rocks. Four smaller rooms are connected to the larger one by "doorways"; the smaller rooms measure 4 m by 2 m, 4 m by 1.5 m, 3.5 m by 1 m, and 1.5 m by 0.8 m. Overall size is 8.5 m by 5.5 m.

The north end of Feature 1 opens to a trail which crosses a cobble-topped low rise; the trail is a cleared strip which varies from 0.5 m to 1.0 m in width. Thirty-five meters from Feature 1, the trail widens into a rectangular area (Feature 2) about 2 m by 1.5 m in size. Like the trail, it is a cleared area. The trail continues past this feature for about 6 m before ending.

No inundation damage was noted at this site.

AZ T:13:28 (PRI-43)

Like AZ T:13:26 west of it, this site (Fig. 4.35) is on a point of the bluff that dominates the study area. This, again, is an obvious place to ascend the bluff, and a prehistoric trail may have passed this way. If so, it has been wiped out by the jeep trail that takes advantage of the same route, and which passes through the center of the site. Further evidence of recent activity includes beer bottle fragments, exploded rifle cartridges, a bullet, and a pop-top to a can.

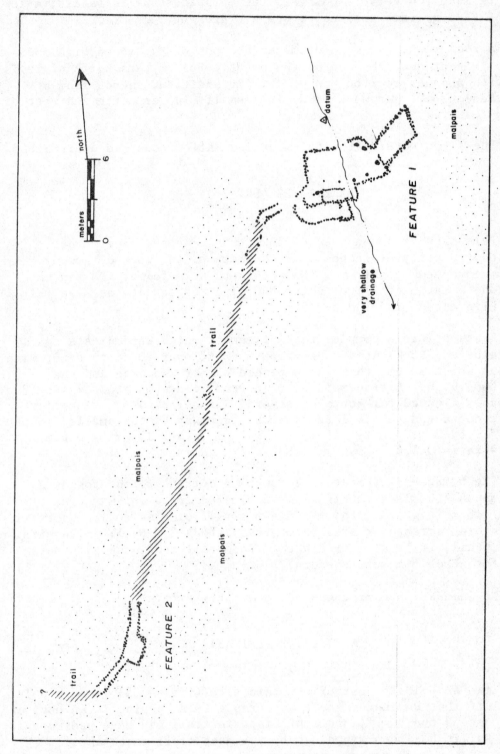

Figure 4.34. AZ T:13:27.

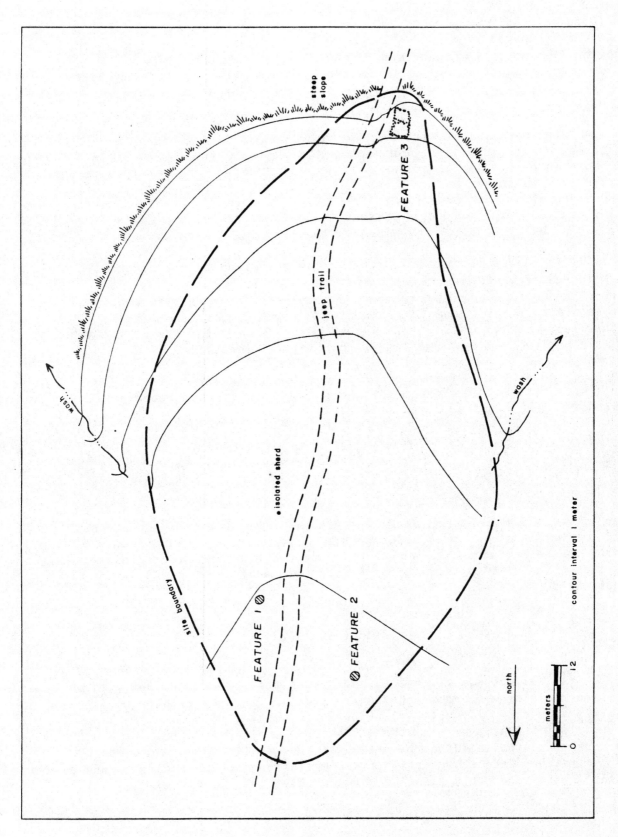

Figure 4.35.   AZ T:13:28.

The site measures 100 m by 55 m, and includes an alignment, sherds, and chipped stone. Multiple use is probable. Feature 1 is a 1-m-diameter cluster of sherds from a Gila Plain, Gila Bend Variety pot. One of the sherds lies several meters outside the cluster. Feature 2 is a 3-m-by-3-m concentration of sherds from a single vessel, probably Salt Red. In addition, an isolated sherd of Lower Colorado Buff Ware (possibly Palomas Buff) was found.

Feature 3, at the tip of the bluff point, is a rectangular alignment measuring 4.5 m (north-south) by 2.5 m (east-west). It is divided in half by an east-west internal alignment. The feature is made of heavily patinated basalt rocks, 10 cm to 40 cm in diameter, set only one high. The interior is fairly clear. No artifacts were found at the alignment itself. Feature 3 is next to the jeep trail, and it is possible that this trail has wiped out part of the alignment.

In addition, the whole site is characterized by a low-density lithic scatter. Cores and flakes of the local basalt are present, as are flakes struck from water-smoothed cobbles of nonlocal, fine-grained stone. A core and two of its flakes were found just south of Feature 1; otherwise, no chipping stations were noted. Perhaps the activities at this site involved tool use rather than initial reduction.

The site is outside the 661-foot inundation zone. Disturbance is limited to the jeep trail and related light scatter of recent trash; much of the site has not been affected by these.

AZ T:13:29 (PRI-63)

This is a 1-m-diameter hearth (Fig. 4.36) in the open desert on top of the bluffs. It contains fire-cracked rocks (up to 20 cm across) and potsherds from a Lower Colorado Buff Ware bowl. No charcoal was noted on the surface. The hearth may extend a few centimeters below the surface. The site is outside the 661-foot inundation zone and is undisturbed.

AZ T:13:30 (PRS-78-22)

AZ T:13:30 was first recorded during the 10-percent survey of the reservoir area (Teague and Baldwin 1978). The site sits on a high, malpais-topped knoll, and is just above the current high water mark. Vegetation is nearly pure creosote bush; one cholla was seen. Within a 35-m-by-25-m area, eight cobble features, one trail segment, one sherd concentration, one lithic artifact concentration, two petroglyphs, and a light scatter of bottle glass were found (Figs. 4.37, 4.38).

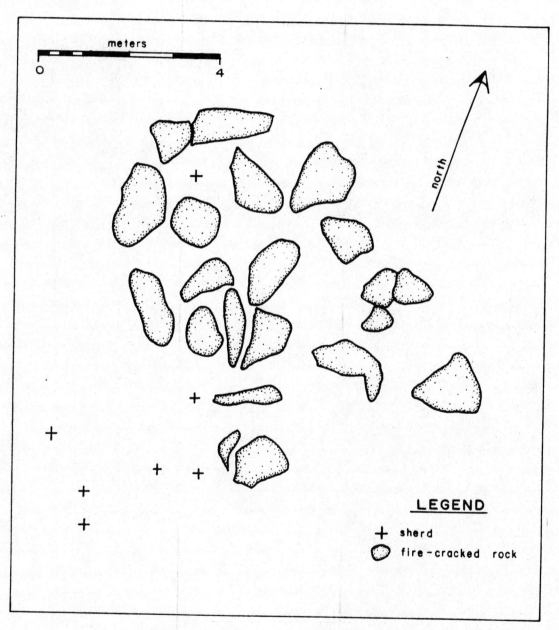

Figure 4.36.   AZ T:13:29.

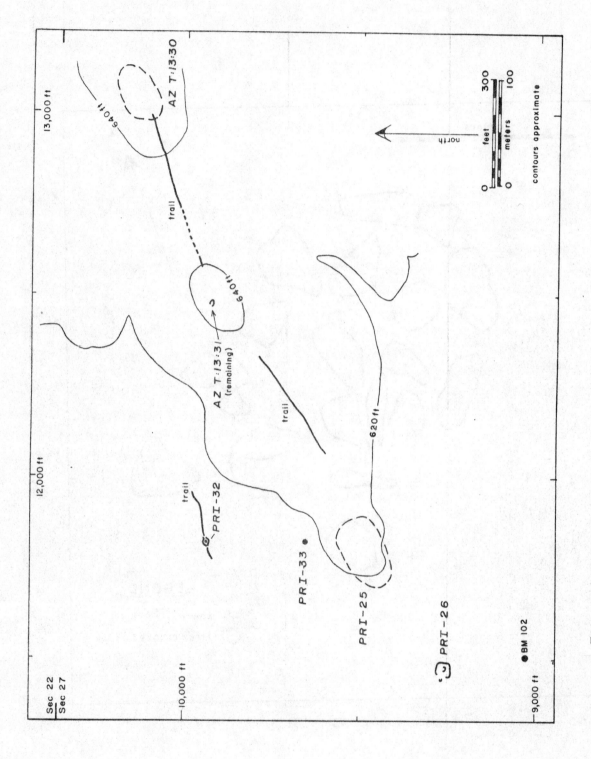

Figure 4.37. AZ T:13:30 and AZ T:13:31; PRI-25, 26, 32, and 33.

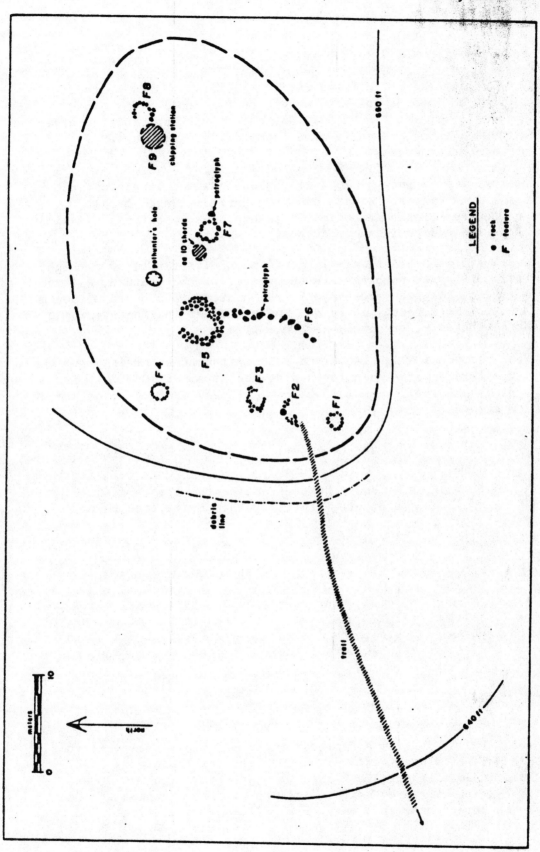

Figure 4.38. AZ T:13:30.

Features

Features 1, 3, 4, 7, and 8 are single-coursed, circular, basalt cobble rings measuring about 1.5 m in diameter. The cobbles from which the rings were made are 10 cm to 40 cm in diameter and show weathering similar to that on cobbles found elsewhere on the knoll. The areas within Features 3, 7, and 8 have been dug out by pot hunters. The areas within Features 1 and 4 are undisturbed and fairly free of gravel in comparison with other areas.

Feature 2 is a partial rock ring whose maximum extension is about 1.5 m. This feature is made of irregularly arranged basalt cobbles and boulders, piled two high in some places, attaining a maximum size of about 1 m. No evidence of vandalism was found.

Feature 5 is a relatively large (4 m in diameter by 50 cm high) circular pile of basalt cobbles. In the center of the feature, a large hole (3 m by 2 m) has been excavated by pot hunters to a depth of 50 cm. Because of this disturbance, it is not known whether the feature was a multi-coursed rock ring or simply a cobble pile.

Feature 6 is a slightly curved rock alignment extending from the southern end of Feature 5 south for a distance of about 10 m. It is made of a single course of about 15 basalt cobbles, most of which are 30 cm to 50 cm across.

Trail

A single trail starts at the west end of the site and once extended to AZ T:13:31 and beyond. Parts of this trail have been destroyed by flooding.

Petroglyphs

A petroglyph was found on a large basalt cobble next to and east of Feature 7. It is a circle connected to a line. A second petroglyph was found on a basalt cobble contained in Feature 6, about 3 m south of Feature 5. Its design is considerably more intricate (Fig. 4.30, see page 50).

Artifacts

About 10 sherds from a Papaguerian brown ware vessel were found within a 2-m-diameter area next to and northwest of Feature 7. A chipping station with about 100 flakes of coarse-textured basalt was found in a 2-m-diameter area next to Feature 8. These appear to come from the same core (not seen); many of the flakes are cortical, and some are up to 20 cm long.

About 10 flakes were found in and around Feature 5, but their morphology suggests that they are the result of pick-axe work in the feature. Green bottle glass with mold seams, probably left by the same pot hunters, was found in and around Feature 5.

Disturbance

In addition to the potholes in Features 3, 5, 7, and 8, a 1.5-m hole was dug northeast of Feature 5. Also, during the 1978 survey, four petroglyphs were reported; we found only two of these. Photographs on file at the Arizona State Museum indicate that one of the two missing petroglyphs was on a large basalt cobble next to the petroglyph we found at Feature 6. Therefore, it seems that the missing petroglyph was removed sometime in the last three years. The fourth petroglyph found in 1978 could not be relocated; it may have been overlooked but more likely has been carried away.

AZ T:13:30 lies above the present floodline and has not been subjected to flooding except for the trail running to AZ T:13:31. Wave action, however, has destroyed the trail in many places.

AZ T:13:31 (PRS-78-23)

AZ T:13:31 lies on a small knoll (Fig. 4.40). It was first reported by Teague and Baldwin (1978). The site is at an elevation of 648 feet, and was just awash at the height of the 1980 flood. The only remains found during the present survey are a partial cobble ring and adjacent chipping station. These are located at the northwest edge of the knoll; this area has been partly cut away by wave action (Fig. 4.41).

Feature 1, the rock ring (Fig. 4.39), consists of basalt cobbles piled three to four rocks high (30 cm to 50 cm). The cobbles are from 10 cm to 30 cm in diameter, show desert varnish, and in some cases have caliche on their undersides. The feature has been sliced in half by the new cut bank. Before this disturbance, the feature probably had an outside diameter of about 2 m and an inside diameter of about 1.3 m (Figs. 4.42, 4.43).

Next to and northeast of Feature 1, about 20 flakes were found in a 1-m-diameter area. All were of coarse-textured basalt, probably from the same core (not found). Many are cortical, and some are very large (up to 20 cm long).

Damage to AZ T:13:31 has been extensive. It is clear from Teague and Baldwin's (1978: 34) site description, and from a pre-inundation aerial photo, that two or three rock rings were present within a 100-square-meter area on the knoll before inundation. With the exception of the remaining half of Feature 1, all traces of these

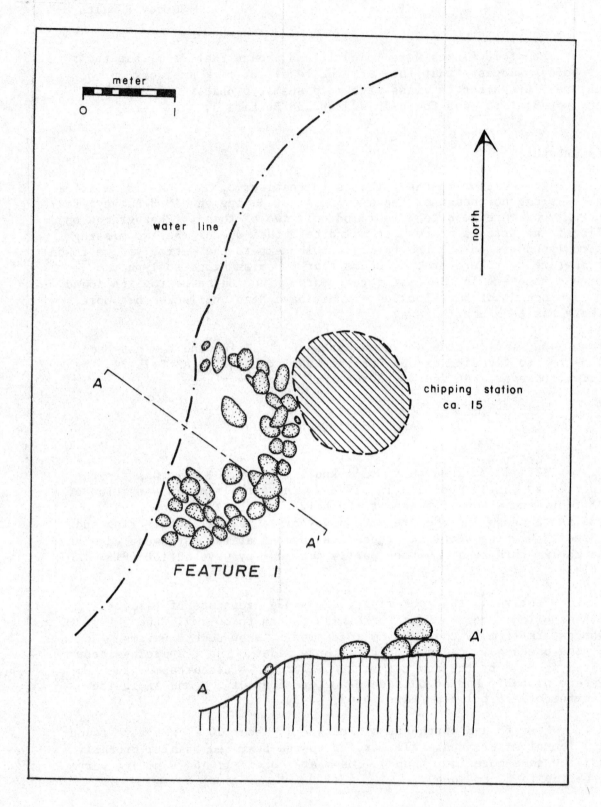

Figure 4.39. AZ T:13:31.

Figure 4.40. AZ T:13:31 and study area from AZ T:13:30.

Figure 4.41. AZ T:13:31 after inundation.

Figure 4.42. AZ T:13:31, Feature 1 before inundation.

Figure 4.43. AZ T:13:31, Feature 1 after inundation.

features (and an unknown quantity of artifacts) were obliterated by the erosion and deposition caused by wave action.

Other Finds

These are reported in the order of their discovery. Breaks in the sequence indicate that the sites already have been described.

PRI-2

This find consists of three rock features and a chipping station just west of AZ T:13:22 (Map 1). Extent of the find is 40 m by 15 m. Feature 1 is a pile of about 10 rocks, and is 50 cm in diameter and 25 cm high. Four meters away is Feature 2, a pile of about 10 rocks; this feature is about 1 m in diameter and 30 cm high. Feature 3 is an irregular rock ring, about 2 m by 1.8 m in size. It is made with cobbles set one or two high and two wide. The interior is about 1.2 m across and is clear. Feature 4 consists of over 50 large basalt flakes in a 2-m-diameter area.

No inundation damage was noted at the site.

PRI-3

A hammerstone of green, nonlocal stone was found next to two noncortical basalt flakes. The hammerstone was heavily battered. No disturbance was noted.

PRI-5

This chipping station consists of about 15 basalt flakes probably struck from the same core (not found). They were found in a 1.5-m-diameter area. No disturbance was noted.

PRI-7

A chipping station, 50 cm by 50 cm in size, included 5 flakes of coarse basalt. Twenty-five meters to the south, an isolated fragment of a basalt core was found. No disturbance was noted.

PRI-8

This find included a chipping station—about 10 basalt flakes within an area 1.5 m by 1 m—and, 25 m to the south, an isolated hammerstone of unidentified, nonlocal, hard stone. No disturbance was apparent.

PRI-10

This hearth (Fig. 4.44) was found on the inside of a bend in a small, intermittent wash; wave damage was extensive and may have removed any associated artifacts. The hearth consists of a low pile of fire-cracked rock about 1 m in diameter and 10 cm high. A small piece of charcoal was seen on the surface; although depth is unknown it cannot be more than a few centimeters.

PRI-11

This rock ring (Fig. 4.45) was found on the edge of a bank next to an intermittent wash. It is 3.5 m by 2.5 m, with an interior of about 1.5 m by 1 m. The ring is made of basalt cobbles piled two or three high and wide.

No artifacts were found in association with this ring. The ring appears to be somewhat tumbled, but there is no way to say when this occurred. Therefore, no inundation-related damage can be discerned.

PRI-13

PRI-13, an isolated hammerstone, is an elongate cobble (about 20 cm long) battered at both ends. It is water-smoothed and is made of nonlocal material. The massiveness of this find is less surprising when one considers the nature of the local chippable stone (coarse-grained basalt) and the size of some of the flakes found in the study area. As stated, however, this find is an isolated one. It is outside the 661-foot inundation zone, and is undisturbed.

PRI-14

Two cores and four flakes were found in a 10-m-by-10-m area. One core is a waterworn cobble of unidentified nonlocal material. The other core is of local basalt, and all four flakes could be refitted to it. The find is outside the 661-foot inundation zone; it is undisturbed.

PRI-15

A basalt cobble (about 20 cm across) had a single flake struck from it; the flake was found 30 cm away. This find is outside the 661-foot inundation zone and is undisturbed.

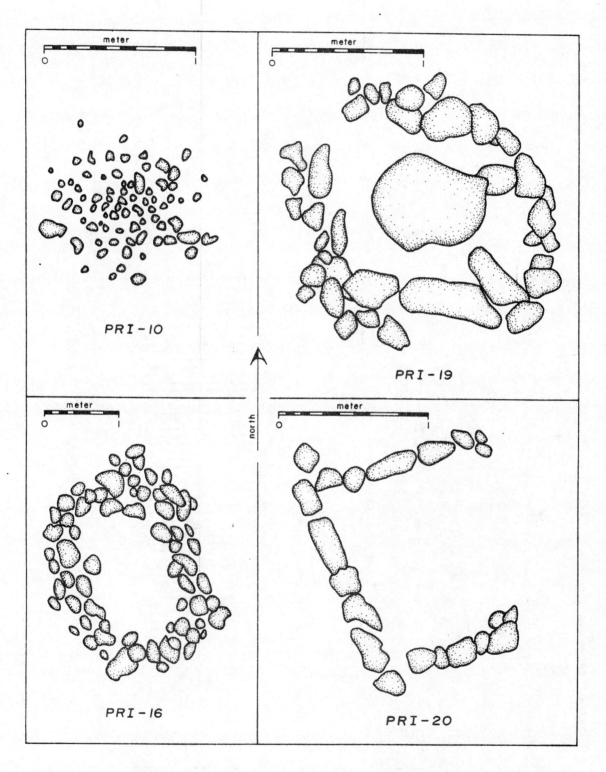

Figure 4.44.   PRI-10, 16, 19, and 20.

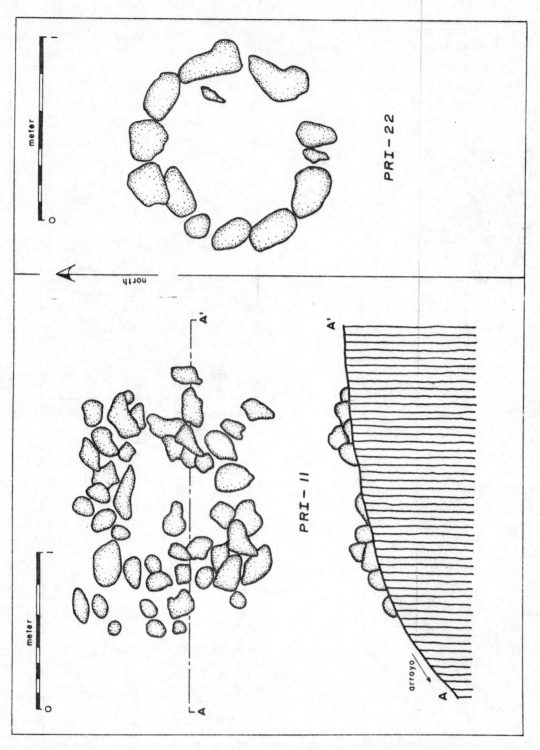

Figure 4.45. PRI-11 and 22.

PRI-16

This isolated rock ring (Fig. 4.44) was found in a silty wash between two, low, malpais-topped rises. It measures 2.5 cm by 1.8 cm, with a clear interior measuring 1.7 m by 1 m. The wall is several cobbles high and wide. No artifacts were found, and no inundation damage was noted.

PRI-17

Two partly cortical flakes of coarse basalt were found 0.5 m apart. No disturbance was noted.

PRI-18

This find consists of an isolated pot break. The original vessel was of Lower Colorado Buff Ware, possibly Patayan II in age. It was an olla about 25 cm in diameter, with a mouth about 8 cm wide. The jar was made with flattened strips of clay; one sherd still has a seam present. No disturbance was noted.

PRI-19

A naturally occurring boulder, 75 cm across, was surrounded by a ring of smaller (20 cm to 40 cm) cobbles; the entire feature is about 2 m by 1.5 m in size (Fig. 4.44). The boulder and ring are in a malpais area. No inundation damage was evident, and no artifacts were seen.

PRI-20

This small alignment is rectilinear, with three sides (Fig. 4.44). It is made of single lines of cobbles 10 cm to 30 cm in diameter. The feature is superficial and has no associated artifacts; no inundation damage could be seen.

PRI-21

This is an isolated core or chopper of nonlocal material, about 15 cm long. It has two unifacial flake scars at one end. It is above the present high-water line; no disturbance was noted.

PRI-22

This hearth ring (Fig. 4.45) is clearly recent. It consists of a simple circle of stones 1.2 m in diameter, and contains charcoal and a bottle neck. Tire tracks were noted 5 m to the east. The feature is undisturbed and is probably post-inundation.

PRI-24

A linear alignment of basalt cobbles (Fig. 4.46) was found in a silty area just off a low, malpais-topped ridge. The alignment is 4.3 m long by 1 m wide, and about 30 cm high. No inundation damage was apparent, and no associated artifacts could be found.

PRI-25

At present, PRI-25 is a low-density scatter of chipped stone. The area has been heavily disturbed by wave action, however, and may originally have been much more substantial. (In addition, a jeep trail once ran through the site.) It is doubtful that the artifacts are in or near their original positions.

The site contains 10 to 20 cores and flakes. One core is of nonlocal quartzite; the other items are of the local basalt.

PRI-26

This feature (Fig. 4.47), one of the larger ones found, is of recent origin. A partial rectangular alignment measures about 10 m by 10 m; it consists of single lines of stones. Just outside the east wall are several fragments of cinder block. Inside the alignment is a much smaller, C-shaped alignment of rocks about 1 m by 2 m in size open to the northwest. This alignment is one or two rocks high and one to three rocks wide. A third (U-shaped) alignment is roughly where one "corner" of the larger alignment would be, if it were present. The U-shaped alignment is also one or two rocks high and one to three rocks wide; it measures 2.5 m by 1.5 m, and is open to the north. Nearby is a bedspring from a steel cot with dimensions suspiciously similar to the third alignment's. Pieces of corrugated tin and other recent trash are scattered in the vicinity of this find.

Some wave action occurred at this feature, and part of the large alignment may have been silted over.

PRI-27

A small, L-shaped alignment (Fig. 4.46) was found east of the labor camp in the study area. The alignment is 1 m long and 30 cm wide, an consists of a single row of small cobbles 10 cm to 15 cm in diameter. Tin cans, glass, and other recent refuse were found nearby. No inundation damage was noted.

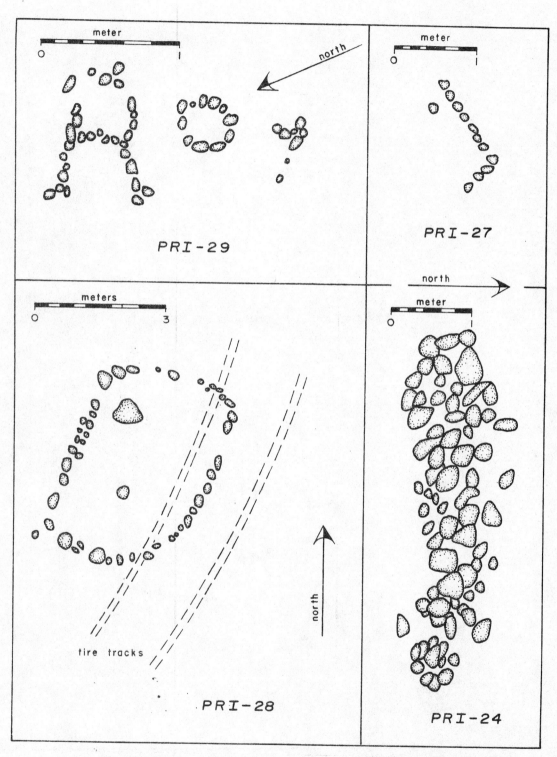

Figure 4.46. PRI-24, 27, 28, and 29.

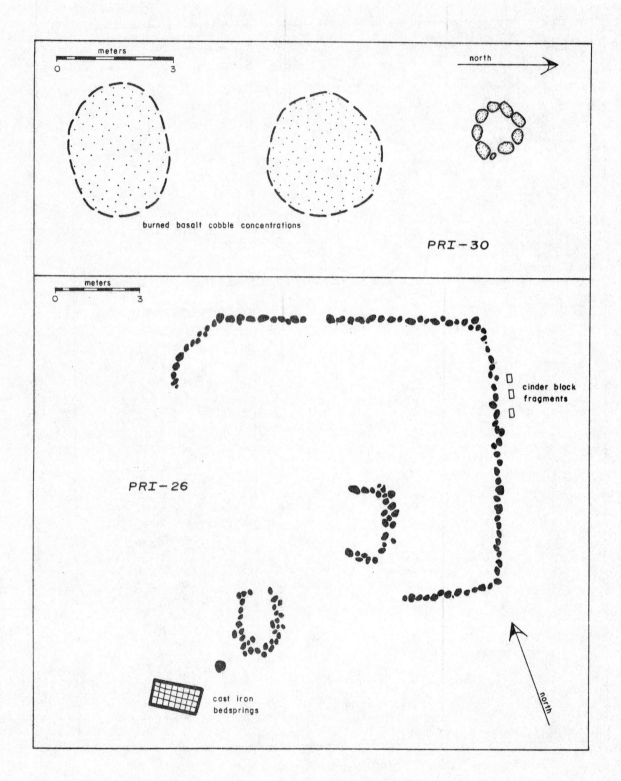

Figure 4.47. PRI-27 and 30.

PRI-28

In the same general area, a subrectangular alignment (Fig. 4.46) and rock pile were found. The alignment consists of a single row of stones, about 25 cm in diameter; it is 5 m long and 3.5 m wide. Except for one large rock, the interior is fairly clear. Nine meters northwest is a rock pile 1.5 m in diameter and 25 cm to 30 cm high. No artifacts were found with these, but recent trash is common in the area.

No inundation damage was noted. A jeep was driven over the subrectangular alignment while the ground was still soft, leaving deep imprints.

PRI-29

Data rarely speak for themselves, but these are an exception (Fig. 4.46). To Roy, wherever you may be, our respectful greetings. No inundation damage was noted. Teague and Baldwin (1978: 30) report initials made with rocks in another part of the reservoir area.

PRI-30

A recent hearth was found at this location (Fig. 4.43); it is about 80 cm in diameter, consists of a simple ring of rocks, and contains charcoal. Tire tracks are present nearby. A few meters south of the hearth two concentrations of cobbles (each about 3 m across) were found. These would not have seemed unusual except for the large amount of thermal spalling (which may indicate use in a fire). No disturbance was noted.

PRI-31

This an isolated core of fine-grained gray basalt, 20 cm in diameter, with three or four flake scars. No disturbance was noted.

PRI-32

This feature (Fig. 4.48) may be an aboriginal alignment reused in recent times. It consists of a rock ring and trail. The ring is 1.5 m in diameter and was originally several courses high. The interior is about 50 cm across and contains ash, charcoal, and nails (indicating the burning of waste lumber).

The ring is in the middle of the trail, which widens around it to form a sort of outer ring about 3 m in diameter. The trail is otherwise about 1 m wide; it extends east and west (Fig. 4.37) to the end of the local malpais cover. No inundation damage was noted.

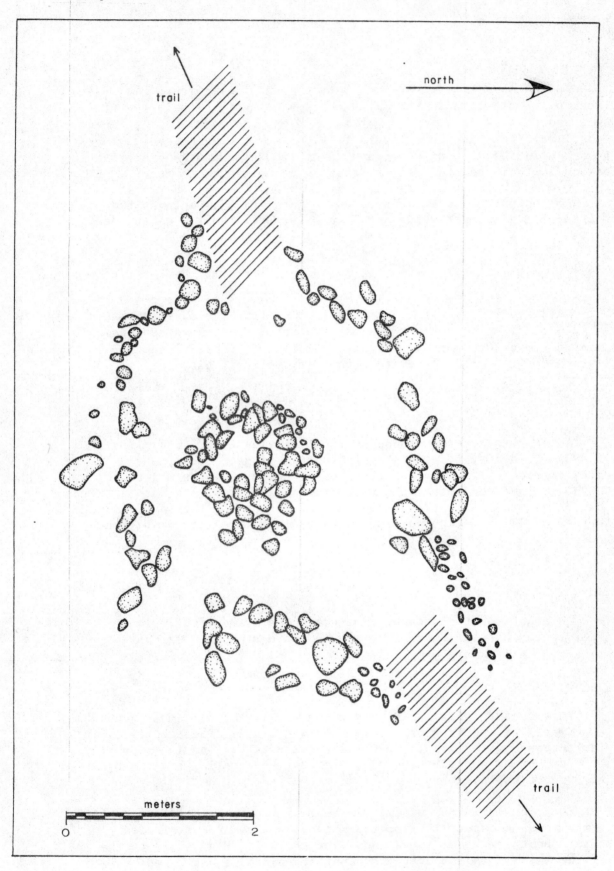

Figure 4.48.   PRI-32.

PRI-33

A small rock ring (Fig. 4.49) was found in a silty draw next to the low ridge on which PRI-25 is located. The ring is 2 m in diameter, with the cleared interior about 1 m across. The least number of rocks (formerly an opening?) is on the northwest side. The ring wall may originally have been about two rocks wide and three to four high; it is now lower and wider. No artifacts were found.

Silt washing into the drainage measures approximately 5 cm to 20 cm in depth at the feature. No inundation damage was noted.

PRI-34

This feature is a small (80-cm-diameter), surficial rock ring made of seven basalt cobbles (Fig. 4.49). It is just off the jeep trail that runs northeast-southwest through the study area. The jeep trail is probably quite recent. No disturbance of the flakes was noted.

PRI-35

A chipping station, PRI-35 contains 6 to 10 pieces of coarse-grained basalt in a 3-m-diameter area. The flakes are 20 cm to 25 cm long. No disturbance was noted.

PRI-36

This find is a cobble of nonlocal quartzite used as a hammerstone (one edge is battered); length is 15 cm. It is outside the 661-foot inundation zone and has not been disturbed.

PRI-37

This find appears to be a mineral or geological test of some kind. A 1-m-wide trail runs from the bottom of the bluff straight to the top, perhaps built to provide access from below. Just off the top edge of the bluff, next to the trail, is a 2-m-by-2-m pit about 1.5 m deep; the spoil is thrown to the sides. No mineralization is present. On top of the bluff, overlooking the pit and trail, is a recent, U-shaped rock hearth, 1 m long and 50 cm wide.

The pit and hearth, and much of the trail, are out of the 661-foot inundation zone. No disturbance was noted.

80 Chapter 4

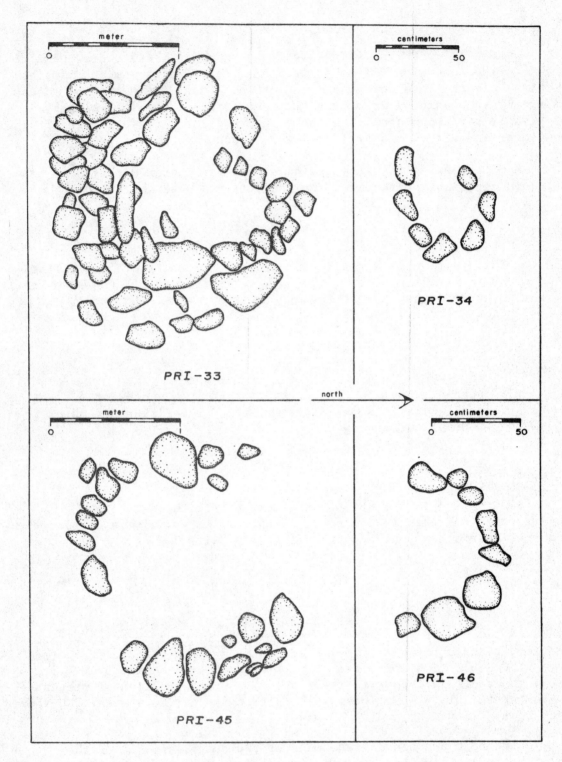

Figure 4.49. PRI-33, 34, 45, and 46.

PRI-38

     A single basalt core was found at this location. It is undisturbed, and is out of the 661-foot inundation zone.

PRI-39

     This is also a core, but of quartzite, which is nonlocal. It is outside the 661-foot inundation zone and is undisturbed.

PRI-40

     This find consists of one unifacial "chopper" or core (of nonlocal material), one unworked cobble (also nonlocal), and a small cairn of basalt rocks. The cairn is made of six rocks and is about 35 cm high; it is 15 m north of the two artifacts, which are 30 cm apart. The find is outside the 661-foot inundation zone and is undisturbed.

PRI-41

     This isolated find is a rectangular, tabular piece of basalt, about 20 cm by 10 cm by 5 cm. It is bifacially chipped along one edge and battered along another. Presumably, it is a tool of some kind. The find is outside the 661-foot inundation area, and has not been disturbed.

PRI-42

     This is a chipping station with 7 to 10 basalt flakes within a 2-m-diameter area. Most likely a single chipping episode happened here. The find is outside the 661-foot inundation zone and is undisturbed.

PRI-44

     An isolated flake of nonlocal igneous stone was found at this spot. It is outside the 661-foot inundation zone and is undisturbed.

PRI-45

     This feature is a 2-m-diameter rock ring made of basalt cobbles 10 cm to 50 cm across (Fig. 4.49). The ring is discontinuous, and is mostly a single row of stones. The interior is fairly clear. No artifacts were found. The feature is outside the 661-foot inundation zone and is undisturbed.

PRI-46

A half-ring of cobbles (Fig. 4.49) was found at the base of a low, malpais-topped rise. The ring is 90 cm across and consists of a single row of rocks, 10 cm to 25 cm in diameter. No artifacts were found, and no inundation damage was noted.

PRI-47

This is a narrow, round bottle (possibly a sauce bottle), 20 cm long and 3.5 cm in diameter, of light green glass. It is marked "71H" on the base. The lack of a neck seam dates it to somewhere before 1920. No disturbance was noted.

PRI-48

At this spot an isolated core of fine-textured stone was found. No disturbance was noted.

PRI-49

Within a 3-m-by-5-m area, two cores and one flake were found. One core appears to be of nonlocal stone; the other core and the flake are of basalt. These items are outside the 661-foot inundation area and are undisturbed.

PRI-50

Five cobbles of hard, nonlocal stone were found lying next to each other. The cobbles are unworked, but similar imported cobbles found in the study area were used for cores. The cobbles are outside the 661-foot inundation zone and are undisturbed.

PRI-51

This chipping station includes about 10 flakes of coarse-grained basalt in a 1-m-by-1-m area. No disturbance was noted. This chipping station is near a trail, as shown in Figure 4.31.

PRI-52

Two basalt flakes were found 0.5 meter apart; no disturbance is apparent. This location is shown in Figure 4.31.

PRI-53

This isolated core of nonlocal, fine-textured stone was found outside the 661-foot inundation zone. No disturbance was noted.

PRI-54

This chipping station contained about 75 flakes (but no core) of vesicular basalt within a 2-m-diameter area. It is outside the 661-foot inundation area; it is undisturbed.

PRI-55

PRI-55, a small chipping station, contained seven flakes of fine-grained silaceous stone in a 5-m-diameter area. This location is outside the 661-foot inundation zone, and no disturbance is apparent.

PRI-56

This find included two small rock piles and a cluster of four basalt flakes. At the edge of a dropoff into a small wash, a pile of 10 to 15 basalt rocks was found, 1 m in diameter and 40 cm high. Forty meters north of the first pile, and slightly farther back from the edge, a second rock pile was found; it is the same size and shape as the first. The four flakes were found in a 1-m-by-1-m area, 25 m north of the first rock pile and more in less in line with the rock piles.

PRI-56 is outside the 661-foot inundation area, and is undisturbed.

PRI-57

This is an isolated rock pile 1 m in diameter and 40 cm high that includes about 10 rocks. It is outside the 661-foot inundation area and has not been disturbed.

PRI-58

A fragmentary, isolated flake of opaque black obsidian was found. It is the only example of this material that we saw in the study area. It is outside the 661-foot inundation zone and is undisturbed.

PRI-59

This chipping station has seven basalt flakes in a 2-m-diameter area. It is outside the 661-foot inundation zone and is undisturbed.

PRI-60

Two flakes of basalt were found 2 m apart. They are outside the inundation area and are undisturbed.

PRI-61

Three basalt flakes were found in a 5-m-by-5-m area. They are outside the 661-foot inundation zone and are undisturbed.

PRI-62

This small cairn, made with four basalt rocks, is 50 cm in diameter and 40 cm high. It is outside the 661-foot inundation zone and is undisturbed.

PRI-64

This chipping station contains 17 basalt flakes in a 1-m-by-1-m area. It is outside the 661-foot inundation area and has not been disturbed.

PRI-65

Two cores were found a meter apart. One is of basalt, the other of unidentified igneous material. The basalt core may have been used as a chopping tool. These are outside the 661-foot inundation area and are undisturbed.

PRI-66

This find consists of a half dozen sherds of Lower Colorado Buff Ware (possibly Colorado Beige) and one flake of local basalt. The area is 1 m by 1 m. The find is outside the 661-foot inundation zone; no disturbance was noted.

PRI-67

This chipping station includes a core and four flakes of basalt in a 2-m-by-2-m area. The four flakes could be refitted to the core, and constituted all the flakes removed. This location is outside the 661-foot inundation zone and is undisturbed.

PRI-68

Two kinds of local basalt were found 0.4 m apart. Each has
continuous unifacial flake removal scars at one end. Possibly these are
chopping tools. They are outside the 661-foot inundation zone and are
undisturbed.

PRI-69

This isolated basalt flake is in an undisturbed area outside the
661-foot inundation zone.

PRI-70

An isolated core (a cobble of quartzite with one flake scar) was
found outside the 661-foot inundation zone; no disturbance was noted.

PRI-71

This isolated basalt flake is in an undisturbed area outside the
661-foot inundation zone.

PRI-72

This chipping station, 1 m in diameter, includes three flakes
and one core of basalt; none of the flakes fits the core. The core may
be a chopping tool. The find is outside the 661-foot inundation zone
and is undisturbed.

PRI-73

A basalt flake was found on the bluff slope; it may have washed
down from above. It is at the edge of the 661-foot inundation zone but
has not been flooded.

PRI-74

This isolated find is a waterworn cobble of nonlocal stone. No
modification is present. It is at the edge of the 661-foot inundation
zone but so far has not been flooded.

PRI-75

Two cores were found here. The first is a waterworn cobble of
igneous (possibly nonlocal) stone, with flakes removed; it may be a

chopping tool. Fifteen meters north is a core of the local basalt.
These are in the 661-foot inundation zone.

PRI-76

Five basalt flakes were found within a 1-m-diameter area. No
disturbance was noted. This chipping station is at the edge of the
661-foot inundation zone.

PRI-77

A basalt core with one flake scar was found beside the flake.
This find, like those before it, is on the bluff slope but presumably in
situ rather than washed down from above. The find is outside the
661-foot inundation zone; no disturbance was noted.

PRI-78

This isolated flake of nonlocal stone is apparently undisturbed.

PRI-79

An isolated medicine bottle of purple glass was found; it is
calibrated for 75 cc. Its color plus the presence of neck seams
indicates a date between 1905 and 1915. It has not been affected by
inundation.

PRI-80

This cairn, 75 cm in diameter and 50 cm tall, corresponds to
point 676 on the USGS quad. Presumably it is a recent survey monument,
but by appearance alone its age is undeterminable. The cairn is outside
the 661-foot inundation zone and is undisturbed.

Other Trails

Before going into the field, we were able to examine
high-altitude, color photos of the study area; these revealed a number of
faint markings which presumably were trails. Figure A.2 in Appendix A
shows the location of those markings. Some proved to be human trails,
but determining the origins of the others presented problems.

The difficult cases were due to two factors. One, of course,
was flooding (which seems to have been more destructive of trails than
of other types of remains). The other was livestock: the study

area is crisscrossed with cow paths, so that any effort to identify
aboriginal routes must distinguish between human paths and bovine ones.
In some cases, bipeds were clearly to blame; in others, we were at a
loss to say whether trails were used by humans, livestock, or both. The
comments that follow, then, are necessarily somewhat limited. Numbers
in parentheses refer to those in Figure A.1.

Human trails show clearly on the high-altitude photo. These
include: the trail from AZ T:13:30 (1) through AZ T:13:31 (2) and
beyond; the trail segment at PRI-32 (3); some of the trails within AZ
T:13:22; the northeast-southwest oriented segment at AZ T:13:23 (4); the
section of trail running north from near AZT:13:24 and 25 (5); and the
section of trail at AZ T:13:27 (14). These have already been described
and illustrated in this chapter. The segment marked (19) is PRI-37, and
those at (18) are cow paths.

Other trail segments were either erased by flooding or were
ambiguous when seen from the ground. The short segment running
northwest from AZ T:13:23 was apparently destroyed by flooding. It is
also possible that this site was connected by a trail to AZ T:13:28
(11), which is on the edge of the bluff dominating the study area. In
the photo, a path runs from AZ T:13:28 south towards AZ T:13:23, but
ends halfway there. Unfortunately, the segment visible in the photo
could not be seen from the ground.

Leading generally northward from AZ T:13:28 is a series of faint
markings. The two most obvious ones are indicated at (11) and (12).
Probably most of these are cow paths, but some might also have seen use
in antiquity.

To the west of this possible trail network is another trail,
which also runs from the edge of the Gila River floodplain to the top of
the bluff. The southern end of the trail (5) is still clearly visible
and is mapped in Figure 4.31. On the aerial photo, the trail can be
traced with a few breaks to the bluff edge at AZ T:13:26 (6), but the
northern portion has been erased by flooding. The trail splits several
times as it climbs the bluff slope, but this may be the work of cows.
The most convincingly man-made segment climbs the bluff just east to AZ
T:13:26. Again, linear features lead north-ward from the bluff edge (7,
8, 10; the last two are outside the study area and were not visited),
but these may also be cow paths.

Between these two networks is a third trail (north-to-south)
that climbs the bluff and then skirts the western edge of a drainage
cutting through the bluff. On the ground it looks like a cow path, but
PRI-14 and PRI-56 were found along it.

On the low-level, aerial photos of AZ T:13:22 and the area just
north of it, a number of faint trails are visible. Except for one trail
(13) that looks cultural, they were probably made by cattle. There are
other isolated segments that might be of human origin (15, 17). Linear

features lying outside the study area can be seen on the aerial photos (for example, 16).

In summary, only limited information on intersite trails could be obtained because of disturbance by flooding and livestock. Given the condition of the trails, it is doubtful that further study could yield much additional information about them.

Survey Results: A Brief Interpretation

A total of 82 finds were made within or adjacent to the study area. The largest of these was AZ T:13:22, or Rock City, which contained 43 features as well as trails, an extensive scatter of lithic artifacts, a thin but equally extensive scatter of historic trash, and a single potsherd.

The features at Rock City consist of basalt cobbles arranged in circles, rectangles, and other forms. While some alignments are made of single rows of rocks, others are more substantial. Size varies as greatly as form. It appears that while some of the alignments are aboriginal, others were made by children from a nearby labor camp.

Rock alignments were also found in other parts of the study area. In general, they remain problematic. PRI-11, on the edge of a wash bank, could be a hunting blind; perhaps other alignments also served this purpose. A number of alignments may be the remains of temporary shelters; candidates for this function are present at AZ T:13:22 (Features 2, 3, 4, 22B, 29, 34, 39, 43, and 47), AZ T:13:23, AZ T:13:25, AZ T:13:30, AZ T:13:31, and PRI-16, PRI-33, and PRI-45.

When other lines of evidence are considered, the picture becomes somewhat clearer. No evidence of permanent settlements was found. Some of the sites probably represent temporary camps: AZ T:13:22, AZ T:13:23, AZ T:13:25 AZ T:13:26, AZ T:13:28, AZ T:13:30, and AZ T:13:31 are the most substantial candidates. These are in "strategic" locations: on the terrace edge next to the Gila floodplain, on the edge of the low bluff dominating the area, or on knolls. Some of them may have seen use in several different periods.

The campsites were probably associated with trails leading away from the Gila floodplain. Whether these merely provided access to backcountry areas or were part of regional travel routes, we do not know.

The study areas were also used as a source of chippable stone; cobbles of basalt were reduced to tools of coarse-grained but adequate material. The limited survey data suggest that both flakes and cores were curated; in some cases, initial preparation of a metate may have occurred. However, the presence of apparently nonlocal stone throughout the area suggests that tool use (and not just procurement) was a factor

here. What that use was, however, remains obscure. Only one piece of
ground stone was found (at AZ T:13:22, Feature 40), and projectile
points are absent; thus the traditional markers of foraging activity are
lacking. Two isolated hearths with fire-cracked rock (AZ T:13:29 and
PRI-10) do suggest food-related activity.

        Chronological evidence is rare. Two sites (AZ T:13:25 and AZ
T:13:26) probably have Preceramic components. Pottery indicates use of
the study area by both Hohokam and Hakataya/Yuma groups. It may also be
noted that the only evidence for European use of the area before 1920 is
two isolated bottles.

        In general, the remains reflect temporary visits to the study
area, presumably from the settlements known to exist in the surrounding
portions of the reservoir area. As such, they form part of the overall
adaptive strategy practiced by ancient peoples of this part of Arizona.

Chapter 5

AGE, SIGNIFICANCE, AND
NATIONAL REGISTER ELIGIBILITY
OF REMAINS

Age of the Finds

As discussed in Chapter 3, many finds were of uncertain age,
being either aboriginal or quite recent. Because this problem bears
directly on their significance, we hoped that an analysis of form would
eventually allow us to isolate early remains.

Some remains, of course, are indisputably aboriginal because
they involve stone-knapping or other non-European practices. These
include AZ T:13:24 and AZ T:13:29; and PRI-3, 5, 7, 8, 10, 13 through
15, 17, 18, 21, 25, 31, 35, 36, 38, 39, 41, 42, 44, 48 through 55, 58
through 61, and 64 through 78. In addition, an aboriginal component (at
least) is present at a number of other sites.

The real problem rests with the rock alignments found. In
trying to determine the age of these features, we looked at the
association between kinds of trash and various alignment forms. The
assumptions were that (1) differences in feature form may be related to
cultural and/or temporal factors, and (2) aboriginal features will tend
to be found with recent trash. We hope that by demonstrating nonrandom
associations of this sort, some useful generalizations about form and
age can be made.

The first step in examining these associations was to devise a
typology of feature form. We began by distinguishing three basic kinds
of features: enclosures, piles, and trails. The piles and trails,
however, were not very distinctive and were not dealt with further. For
enclosures, it was possible to define four binary attributes, all
assumed to be equally important:

1. Size--Enclosures were grouped as small (less than 2 m
   across) or large (more than 2 m across).
2. Internal structure--Enclosures whose interiors were not
   partitioned were called "simple," while those whose
   interiors were subdivided were termed "complex."
3. Shape--Enclosures were described as being either curvilinear
   or rectilinear.

4. Number of courses--Enclosures made of only one course of
   cobbles were distinguished from those with more than one
   course of cobbles.

When these attributes were applied to enclosures in the study
area, 11 "types" resulted:

     I. small, simple, curvilinear, single-coursed
    II. small, simple, curvilinear, multi-coursed
   III. large, simple, curvilinear, single-coursed
    IV. large, simple, curvilinear, multi-coursed
     V. small, complex, curvilinear, multi-coursed
    VI. large, complex, curvilinear, multi-coursed
   VII. large, complex, rectilinear, single-coursed
  VIII. small, simple, rectilinear, single-coursed
    IX. large, simple, rectilinear, single-coursed
     X. large, complex, rectilinear, multi-coursed
    XI. large, simple, rectilinear, multi-coursed

In addition, a twelfth "type," termed "other," was established
to accommodate PRI-29 ("ROY"). Frequencies for these types are given by
site in Table 5.1.

When the occurrence of prehistoric and historic artifacts with
enclosure types was examined, no patterns could be demonstrated. This
suggests that the assumption that features would be associated with
broadly contemporaneous artifacts is unrealistic. Rather, it seems
likely that reuse of the area in historic times created spurious
associations between prehistoric features and recent trash, and possibly
equally spurious associations between prehistoric artifacts and recent
features. In short, attempts at feature dating through trash
associations were unsuccessful.

A second approach to distinguishing early from recent features
was based on the assumptions that (1) differences in feature form are
related to temporal factors, and (2) prehistoric and historic features
may be distributed differently in space. In particular, since the
recent alignments were probably made by children from the old labor camp
in the study area, it seems reasonable to assume that those features
would tend to be near the camp. (Aboriginal features, in contrast,
would be more evenly distributed across the landscape.) To investigate
this possibility, enclosure types were compared for those sites near the
labor camp (AZ T:13:22, and PRI-2, 26, 27, 29, 32, and 33) and those
farther away (all other alignments). The results are shown in Table
5.2.

Given sample size and quality, prudence dictates against
involved statistical analysis of the results. Nonetheless, some
tendencies in the data can be noted.

First, it appears that the area surrounding the abandoned labor
camp is more heterogeneous than the rest of the study area. This is to

Table 5.1

DISTRIBUTIONS OF ENCLOSURES BY STYLE

Site	\multicolumn{12}{c}{Enclosure Type}
	I	II	III	IV	V	VI	VII	VIII	IX	X	XI	XII
T:13:22	6	3	1	7	1	0	6	2	3	2	1	0
T:13:23	1	-	1	-	-	-	-	-	-	-	-	-
T:13:25	-	-	-	1	-	-	-	-	-	-	-	-
T:13:26	1	-	-	-	-	-	-	-	-	-	-	-
T:13:27	-	-	-	-	-	-	1	-	-	-	1	-
T:13:28	-	-	-	-	-	-	1	-	-	-	-	-
T:13:30	5	1	-	-	-	-	-	-	-	-	-	-
T:13:31	-	-	-	1	-	-	-	-	-	-	-	-
PRI-2	-	-	-	1	-	-	-	-	-	-	-	-
PRI-11	-	1	-	-	-	-	-	-	-	-	-	-
PRI-16	-	-	-	1	-	-	-	-	-	-	-	-
PRI-19	-	1	-	-	-	-	-	-	-	-	-	-
PRI-20	-	-	-	-	-	-	-	1	-	-	-	-
PRI-22	1	-	-	-	-	-	-	-	-	-	-	-
PRI-26	-	-	-	-	-	-	-	-	1	-	2	-
PRI-27	-	-	-	-	-	-	-	1	-	-	-	-
PRI-29	-	-	-	-	-	-	-	-	-	-	-	1
PRI-32	-	-	-	-	1	-	-	-	-	-	-	-
PRI-33	-	1	-	-	-	-	-	-	-	-	-	-
PRI-34	1	-	-	-	-	-	-	-	-	-	-	-
PRI-45	1	-	-	-	-	-	-	-	-	-	-	-
PRI-46	1	-	-	-	-	-	-	-	-	-	-	-

Note: AZ T:13:22, Features 5 and 42, and PRI-28 are excluded because they are ambiguous with respect to shape.
AZ T:13:23, Features 2 and 3, and AZ T:13:30, Feature 5 are excluded because they are too heavily disturbed to determine form.

Table 5.2

DISTRIBUTION OF ENCLOSURES RELATIVE TO LABOR CAMP

Enclosure Type	At Sites Near Labor Camp		At Sites Some Distance From Labor Camp	
	Number	Percent	Number	Percent
I	6	14.6	11	50.0
II	3	7.2	4	18.2
III	1	2.4	1	4.5
IV	9	22.0	2	9.1
V	1	2.4	--	--
VI	1	2.4	--	--
VII	6	14.6	2	9.1
VIII	3	7.3	1	4.5
IX	5	12.2	--	--
X	2	4.9	--	--
XI	3	7.3	1	4.5
XII	1	2.4	--	--
Totals	41	100.0	22	100.0

be expected if aboriginal and recent alignments occur together near the camp. Second, using the same spatial distinctions, some differences related to size and shape can be seen (Table 5.3). Enclosures near the old labor camp are more commonly large or rectilinear, while enclosures at a greater distance have a strong tendency to be small or curvilinear. Single versus multiple coursing, and simple versus complex alignments, show less divergence.

Table 5.3
ENCLOSURE CHARACTERISTICS RELATIVE TO LOCATION
(PRI-29 is excluded)

Enclosure Type	At Sites Near Labor Camp		At Sites Some Distance From Labor Camp	
	Number	Percent	Number	Percent
1. Curvilinear	21	52.5	18	81.8
Rectilinear	19	47.5	4	18.2
Totals	40	100.0	22	100.0
2. Small	13	32.5	16	72.7
Large	27	67.5	6	27.3
Totals	40	100.0	22	100.0
3. Simple	30	75.0	20	90.9
Complex	10	25.0	2	9.1
Totals	40	100.0	22	100.0
4. Single-coursed	21	52.5	15	68.2
Multi-coursed	19	47.5	2	31.8
Totals	40	100.0	22	100.0

A fairly strong tendency can be isolated by combining two of the binary attributes just reviewed. Table 5.4 shows that large, rectilinear enclosures are common near the camp, but rare elsewhere. It is interesting in this regard that all five large, simple, rectilinear, single-coursed enclosures (Type IX) are near the camp.

Unfortunately, these data do not yield any absolute criteria for distinguishing old from new alignments. As counter-examples, the probable aboriginal alignment at AZ T:13:28 is rectilinear, and Teague and Baldwin (1978: 30) report a circular alignment made of chunks of concrete. In the end, the trends noted are nothing more than trends.

Table 5.4
DISTRIBUTION OF LARGE RECTILINEAR
VERSUS OTHER ENCLOSURES

Enclosure Type	At Sites Near Labor Camp		At Sites Some Distance From Labor Camp	
	Number	Percent	Number	Percent
Large Rectilinear Enclosures	16	40.0	3	13.6
Other Enclosures	24	60.0	19	86.4
Totals	40	100.0	22	100.0

Perhaps they will help future workers sort out old and new alignments, as comparative samples become available.

This conclusion, however, leaves the problem of assigning dates to the alignments. With no guidelines to go by, the safest approach seems to be to create a series of age "classes," each keyed to the quality of evidence available. Thus the somewhat intuitive assignments that follow will at least leave the door open for future criticism and revisions. The classes are:

I. Clearly Ancient These are in close association with aboriginal remains; there is no reason to suspect recent activity. The alignments in question are AZ T:13:23, 25, 26, 30, and 31.

II. Probably Ancient

1. Alignments associated with aboriginal remains; recent activity could account for alignments but this is doubtful. Alignments are found at AZ T:13:28, and PRI-40 and PRI-56.
2. Alignments not associated with aboriginal remains, but similar to aboriginal alignments commonly found elsewhere; no reason to suspect recent activity. These alignments are found at PRI-11, 16, 45, and 57.
3. Alignments where recent activity is a possibility but similar to aboriginal alignments commonly found elsewhere; probably "too substantial" to be child's play. These are PRI-33, and AZ T:13:22, Features 2, 3, 4, 22B, 29, 34, 39,

43, 44, and 47. (At Feature 29, the external walls may be ancient, the internal alignments recent.)

III. Ambiguous

1. Alignments where there is no evidence of recent activity, but which do not resemble common aboriginal alignments and which are not associated with aboriginal artifacts. These are AZ T:13:27, and PRI-19 and PRI-20.
2. Alignments where recent activity may account for construction, and with shapes that could be either aboriginal or recent; not "too substantial" for child's play. These are PRI-2, 24, 46, and 62; and AZ T:13:22, Features 5, 8, 13, 14, 15, 16, 17B, 20, 22A, 24, 26, 28A, 28B, 35B, 36, 37, 40, 42, 48, and 50.
3. Alignments at T:13:22 that are rectilinear; mostly single-coursed. Based on the previous discussion, these could conceivably be classed as recent, but any such classification would be tenuous. They include Features 10, 11, 17A, 23, 30, 33, 35A, 38, 41, and 45.
4. These sites have clear recent components, but may be ancient loci reused recently. They are PRI-30 and PRI-32.

IV. Probably Recent Form, extent, and association with recent remains suggest a recent origin for these finds. Moreover, they are not "too substantial" to have been created by playing children. They are PRI-26, 27, 28, 34, and 80 (this last being a probable survey marker). Also, AZ T:13:22, Feature 6 can be placed here--it is probably a play "house," with "dining room table" and four surrounding "chairs," plus other "rooms" (Figure 4.2).

V. Clearly Recent Form, extent, technology, or associations leave no doubt as to the recent origin of these features. They include AZ T:13:22, Feature 1; and PRI-22, 29, 37, 47, and 79. (The last two are bottles that are over 50 years old.)

At the end of all this we cannot help but believe that far too many alignments remain undated, and that the dating for many others is somewhat shaky. The common euphemism for such circumstances is, "More work is needed." However, more intensive study of the same features is not, of itself, likely to be the best approach in terms of cost or information return. The alignments are ambiguous because they are superficial, undistinctive in many cases, and lacking in demonstrably associated artifacts--qualities that do not lend themselves to intensive research. For now, some sort of limited testing would probably be most appropriate (and is recommended in Chapter 6).

It may turn out, however, that the real key to the ambiguous alignments will be comparative data. Comparisons of form over greater areas may yield much sharper trends than were discernable within the confines of the study area. The needed data must come, in part, from future work in the Painted Rock Reservoir area; in other words, a "wait-and-see" approach may be best. This can be suggested in part because the ambiguous alignments do not seem to be in immediate danger of destruction by flooding. Of course, it means that some of the remains managed in this way will later turn out to be recent; but it seems wiser to do this than to ignore a number of possibly ancient remains--or to spend a lot of effort in potentially frustrating intensive studies.

Significance of the Finds

The discussion just presented can now be applied to evaluating the significance of the remains found. Recent, ambiguous, and ancient remains will be dealt with in turn.

Recent Remains

Finds identified as "Clearly Recent" or "Probably Recent" can be considered less than 50 years old and not significant (again, with the exception of PRI-47 and PRI-79).

Ambiguous Remains

Because of the age of these remains, it is not possible to assess their potential significance. While this in itself might be construed as an argument against their significance, ignoring them could eventually lead to a significant loss of archaeological information.

For that reason, it is probably best to consider them as potentially significant; in time the distinction between recent and ancient remains should become clearer.

Early Remains

These include those alignments classed as "Clearly Ancient" or "Probably Ancient," PRI-47 and 79, and all the sites listed at the beginning of the chapter. Such remains are not automatically significant; here we will consider a second criterion of significance, the ability of sites to yield important information about problems in archaeology or prehistory. It seems appropriate here to cite recent comments by the Heritage Conservation and Recreation Service (in GAO 1981): "Certainly all sites contain information, but the key question is whether that information is important enough to preserve and protect the site and/or the information it contains for future generations."

It can be argued that a site is "important enough" when it is likely to help fill in serious gaps in the known cultural and adaptive history of a local area or region. Sites in the study area promise to do just that. Formerly, research at Painted Rock has focused on large sites; we are only beginning to get a picture of what went on in "hinterland" areas--and of the role of smaller sites and special activity loci in the lives of people who lived at Painted Rock.

Moreover, with two possible Preceramic sites located, there is a chance to extend the Painted Rock sequence back through time. It is noteworthy that, so far, not a single Preceramic site has been positively identified in the reservoir area, even though this period lasted at least 10,000 years in the greater Southwest.

These examples should make it clear that much basic information remains to be gathered for the Gila Bend area, and that the sites located by this study can help answer the questions. It is true that with a more thorough understanding of what remains are present at Painted Rock--and of local culture history--some of these sites would probably seem less important. However, lacking that information, we can only suppose that the sites could be important, and in some cases unique, representatives of ancient periods or practices.

Eligibility for the National Register

Because the remains found are significant in the sense just given, they are potentially eligible for nomination to the National Register of Historic Places. Any such determination, however, should probably be in terms of a district. First, none of the sites alone is an outstanding source of cultural information. Second, and related, is that the finds seem to be most easily understood as parts of a greater whole.

A quick review of the finds may serve to illustrate the first point. AZ T:13:22 contains an ancient component, but there are problems in isolating that component given recent activity. AZ T:13:23 is clearly aboriginal but has been disturbed by inundation. Disturbance is also a problem at AZ T:13:24, which in addition is a special activity site with few remains. AZ T:13:25 may be Preceramic, but only one rock ring and some chipped stone are present. AZ T:13:26 also contains probable Preceramic remains, but all the chipped stone seen would probably fit into a shoebox. AZ T:13:27 lacks artifacts and cannot be positively dated. AZ T:13:28 is extensive but has a low density of remains; it is partly disturbed by a jeep trail. AZ T:13:29 is an isolated hearth; AZ T:13:30 has been disturbed by pot hunters; and AZ T:13:31 has been almost completely destroyed. Other finds are less substantial, and by themselves do not come close to qualifying for nomination. While it might be possible to establish eligibility for two or three of the finds, the actual majority of remains would be overlooked by a site-by-site evaluation.

The second point is equally compelling. Unlike many large sites, chipping stations, trails, rock alignments, and temporary camps reflect only a small part of a given adaptive pattern. Each of these types of sites is best understood in terms of the other types and the relationships among them. Adequate management may not mean protection or mitigation work for all such sites; but the full range of variability, and its greater implications, should at least be considered.

In sum, the study area is characterized by a "low-density" archaeology in which the nature and distribution of remains calls for an areal rather than site-by-site approach. Moreover, in taking such an approach it would appear that the remains found are sufficiently important to warrant a determination of eligibility for nomination to the National Register.

Chapter 6

RECOMMENDATIONS AND CONCLUSIONS

The study area described in this report contains a number of
clearly significant archaeological remains, plus other loci of possible
significance but of uncertain age and cultural affiliation. Each
find--and the apparent impact of flooding on that find--has been
discussed in detail in Chapter 5; that information is summarized in
Table 6.1. Locational data, which are potentially sensitive, are given
in Appendix A.

For the most part, no further research is needed to determine
location, areal extent, depth of deposits, and significance of cultural
resources in the study area; that information is contained in this
report. In some cases it was not possible to determine the age of
remains, but we do not recommend additional investigation solely to
resolve this problem (see the sections on dating and significance in
Chapter 5). Instead, we recommend that these remains be managed along
with "Clearly Ancient" remains, as part of the monitoring and testing
program discussed below. Data from this program may clear up some
ambiguities; comparative data from future studies in other parts of the
reservoir area may provide the additional information needed to
understand the alignments in question. As more information becomes
available, the Corps of Engineers should be able to determine the age of
previously ambiguous features, and to act accordingly.

The significance of remains that are "Clearly Ancient"
derives from the cultural resources as a whole, rather than from
individual sites. Therefore, we consider the remains eligible for
nomination to the National Register as a district.

A number of significant remains have been adversely affected by
the operation of Painted Rock Reservoir, and they will continue to be
adversely affected. The section that follows attempts to describe, in
general terms, the effect of flooding on sites in the study area. With
this information as background, the remainder of the chapter presents
specific recommendations for a mitigation program.

Effects of Inundation: Some General Comments

The study of archaeological sites within reservoir areas is
still at a formative stage (Lenihan and others 1977, Carrell and others
1976, Garrison 1975). However, some working assumptions already exist

101

Table 6.1

CULTURAL RESOURCES: EXTENT, TYPE,

CONDITION, AND RECOMMENDATIONS

Site Number	Horizontal Extent (m)	Depth (cm) S = less than 5 cm	Type, Complexity, etc.	Condi-tion	Recommendations		
					No Action	Monitor	Excavate/ Collect
AZ T:13:22 (PRI-1, (PRS-78-16)	240 x 320	0-10	"Rock City." 43 rock alignment features and many trail segments, chipped stone scatter and concentrations; 1 sherd. Multiple use, including aboriginal and recent.	good-fair		X	
AZ T:13:23 (PRI-4)	50 x 30?	S	Campsite? Rock alignments and section of trail; chipped stone; petroglyphs.	poor			X
AZ T:13:24 (PRI-6)	135 x 45	S	12 chipping stations and scatter of chipped stone	poor			X
AZ T:13:25 (PRI-9)	20 x 10	S	Sleeping circle; chipped stone. Possibly preceramic	fair			X
AZ T:13:26 (PRI-12)	55 x 20	S	Campsite? Rock ring. Chipped stone. Probably multiple use with prece-ramic components	good	X		
AZ T:13:27 (PRI-23)	55 x 15	S	2 rock alignments and connecting trail	good		X	
AZ T:13:28 (PRI-43)	100 x 55	S	Rock alignment; pottery; chipped stone. Probably multiple use	fair	X		
AZ T:13:29 (PRI-63)	1 x 1	5-10	Hearth with pottery	good	X		
AZ T:13:30 (PRS-78-22)	35 x 25	S	Campsite? 7 stone rings and 1 linear feature; petroglyphs; pottery; chipped stone; trail	fair			X
AZ T:13:31 (PRS-78-23)	5 x 5	S	Campsite? Originally 2-3 rock circles, trail, chipped stone. At present, part of 1 circle, 1 chip-ping station remain	poor			X
PRI-2	40 x 15	S	2 rock piles; rock ring; chipping station	good		X	

Table 6.1. (continued)

Site Number	Horizontal Extent (m)	Depth (cm) S = less than 5 cm	Type, Complexity, etc.	Condition	Recommendations		
					No Action	Monitor	Excavate/Collect
PRI-3	1 x 1	S	Hammerstone and 2 flakes	good	X		
PRI-5	2 x 2	S	Chipping station.	good			X
PRI-7	1 x 1	S	Chipping station	good			X
PRI-8	25 x 2	S	Chipping station; isolated hammerstone	good			X
PRI-10	1 x 1	0-15	Isolated hearth	poor			X
PRI-11	2 x 2	S	Isolated rock ring	good		X	
PRI-13	n.a.	S	Isolated hammerstone	good	X		
PRI-14	10 x 10	S	Chipping station	good	X		
PRI-15	1 x 1	S	Core and flake	good	X		
PRI-16	3 x 2	S	Isolated rock ring	good		X	
PRI-17	1 x 1	S	2 flakes	good	X		
PRI-18	1 x 1	S	Pot break	good		X	
PRI-19	2 x 2	S	Rock ring and boulder	good		X	
PRI-20	2 x 2	S	Rectangular alignment	good		X	
PRI-21	n.a.	S	Isolated core or chopper	good	X		
PRI-22	1 x 1	S	Recent hearth	good	X		
PRI-24	4 x 1	S	Rock alignment	good		X	
PRI-25	100 x 75	S	Very low density scatter of chipped stone	poor			X
PRI-26	15 x 15	S	Recent rock alignments and trash	fair	X		
PRI-27	1 x 1	S	Recent (?) rock alignment	good	X		
PRI-28	15 x 5	S	Rock alignment and rock pile	fair	X		

Table 6.1. (continued)

Site Number	Horizontal Extent (m)	Depth (cm) S = less than 5 cm	Type, Complexity, etc.	Condition	Recommendations		
					No Action	Monitor	Excavate/ Collect
PRI-29	2 x 1	S	Recent rock alignment	good	X		
PRI-30	40 x 10	S	Recent hearth; 2 cobble concentrations with possible heat-altered rock	good		X	
PRI-31	n.a.	S	Isolated core	good	X		
PRI-32	75 x 5	S	Hearth with recent contents. Trail	good		X	
PRI-33	2 x 2	5-20	Rock ring	good		X	
PRI-34	1 x 1	S	Small rock circle; probably recent	good	X		
PRI-35	3 x 3	S	Chipping station	good		X	
PRI-36	n.a.	S	Isolated hammerstone	good	X		
PRI-37	150 x 20	S	Minerals (?) test, hearth; trail (?). Recent	good	X		
PRI-38	n.a.	S	Isolated core	good	X		
PRI-39	n.a.	S	Isolated core	good	X		
PRI-40	15 x 1	S	Small rock pile; core/chopper; non-local cobble	good	X		
PRI-41	n.a.	S	Isolated chipped stone tool	good	X		
PRI-42	2 x 2	S	Chipping station	good	X		
PRI-44	n.a.	S	Isolated flake	good	X		
PRI-45	2 x 2	S	Rock circle	good	X		
PRI-46	1 x 1	S	Rock semicircle	good		X	
PRI-47	n.a.	S	Glass bottle. Pre-1920.	good	X		
PRI-48	n.a.	S	Isolated core	good	X		

Table 6.1.   (continued)

Site Number	Horizontal Extent (m)	Depth (cm) S = less than 5 cm	Type, Complexity, etc.	Condi-tion	Recommendations		
					No Action	Monitor	Excavate/Collect
PRI-49	5 x 3	S	2 cores and 1 flake	good	X		
PRI-50	1 x 1	S	5 unworked, non-local cobbles	good	X		
PRI-51	1 x 1	S	Chipping station	good		X	
PRI-52	1 x 1	S	2 flakes	good	X		
PRI-53	n.a.	S	Isolated core	good	X		
PRI-54	2 x 2	S	Chipping station	good	X		
PRI-55	5 x 5	S	Chipping station	good	X		
PRI-56	40 x 5	S	2 rock piles; chipping station	good	X		
PRI-57	1 x 1	S	Rock pile	good	X		
PRI-58	n.a.	S	Isolated flake	good	X		
PRI-59	2 x 2	S	Chipping station	good	X		
PRI-60	2 x 1	S	2 flakes	good	X		
PRI-61	2 x 1	S	3 flakes	good	X		
PRI-62	n.a.	S	Small rock pile	good	X		
PRI-64	1 x 1	S	Chipping station	good	X		
PRI-65	1 x 1	S	2 cores	good	X		
PRI-66	1 x 1	S	Pot break, 1 flake	good	X		
PRI-67	1 x 1	S	Chipping station	good	X		
PRI-68	1 x 1	S	2 cores or choppers	good	X		
PRI-69	n.a.	S	Isolated flake	good	X		
PRI-70	n.a.	S	Isolated core	good	X		
PRI-71	n.a.	S	Isolated flake	good	X		

Table 6.1. (continued)

Site Number	Horizontal Extent (m)	Depth (cm) S = less than 5 cm	Type, Complexity, etc.	Condi-tion	Recommendations		
					No Action	Monitor	Excavate/Collect
PRI-72	1 x 1	S	Chipping station	good	X		
PRI-73	n.a.	S	Isolated flake	good	X		
PRI-74	n.a.	S	Isolated cobble, non-local material	good	X		
PRI-75	15 x 1	S	2 cores	good	X		
PRI-76	1 x 1	S	Chipping station	good		X	
PRI-77	n.a.	S	Core and flake	good	X		
PRI-78	n.a.	S	Isolated flake	good	X		
PRI-79	n.a.	S	Glass bottle. 1905-1915	good	X		
PRI-80	1 x 1	S	Rock pile. Probably recent	good	X		

that can be applied to the study area. Factors that determine the integrity of flooded resources include:

1. Nature of the remains. Lenihan and others (1977: 21-30) predicted that "low-lying rubble of stone" and "lithic and/or ceramic surface scatter" would be little affected by flooding in the absence of heavy currents and surface erosion. For the most part, this was true; rock alignments themselves tended to be minimally disturbed, and pottery and chipped stone concentrations were still identifiable. It is possible that chipped stone will become less useful for microanalysis after flooding (Lenihan and others 1977: 30-36, 68); but since the study area's chipped stone is primarily of coarse basalt and is probably mostly reduction debris, this is not a serious problem.

    It is likely, however, that any living surfaces associated with the alignments were damaged by flooding--for example, the interiors of Features 2 and 3 at Rock City. The soil there shrank as it dried, creating a web of mud cracks at least 5 cm deep. Any floors in those two features were either damaged or destroyed. Similar cracking took place to lesser degrees wherever alignments trapped floodwaters.

    An additional danger to living surfaces is created by the propagation of salt cedar by flooding:

    > Saltcedar root disturbance may exert a highly destructive force upon archaeological sites. Although the natural plant community [at Painted Rock] is composed of large shrubs and trees, such as paloverde and mesquite, it is very openly spaced under natural hydrological and climatic conditions. The effects of root disturbance by the original plant community seems to be much less destructive than that in present introduced saltcedar situations.

    > The possible impacts upon sites, by not only saltcedar, but also by other vegetational changes caused by inundation, should be thoroughly evaluated (Lenihan and others 1977: 235).

    Finally, as discussed earlier, trails seem more susceptible to flood damage than rock alignments or artifact scatters.

2. Nature of the substrate. In general, gravels or gravel/sand mixtures should be resistant to mechanical processes of

flooding (Lenihan and others 1977: 20). In the study area,
however, several aspects of the local substrate affected our
ability to interpret finds.

The first was alteration of the natural ground
covering. Originally, the basalt rocks in the study area
had a naturally dark cortex and sometimes a coat of desert
varnish; the ground surface between them was often covered
by large, crumblike, solid particles. Whenever these were
cleared away to create a feature or trail, the contrast
between them and the lighter soil beneath made such features
obvious. Flooding has either "bleached" the rocks or given
them a white coating, and the coarse "crumbs" have now been
reworked into highly localized beach deposits. As a result,
cleared areas no longer stand out--especially in the case of
trails.

An associated problem was caliche removal. The
caliche found on many rocks in alignments was one possible
clue to their age. It is noteworthy that at least some of
this material survived its recent baths; but we suspect that
some was dissolved. (More precise statements would require
some sort of before-and-after measurements.) Thus, at least
one source of information on the age of sites may be
disappearing. Identifying caliche coating on rocks was also
complicated by the fact that the tops of rocks are now as
pallid as their bottoms. This must also mean that
petroglyphs are affected, though one was found at a
previously submerged site (AZ T:13:23).

3. Slope. Slope does not seem to have been much considered in
inundation studies, but it is critical in this case. The
sites or features which escaped heavy damage were, in
general, on flat to gently sloping ground; those on slopes
of more than roughly 3 degrees, or on knolls or rises, were
usually severely affected by flooding.

The principal agent is wave action. Even though
it was not strong enough to move rocks, it did erode the
soil around them, allowing the unsupported rocks to
tumble away. It is unclear why the effects of wave action
were most intense on slopes, but such areas saw the greatest
amount of cut bank and beach formation. Rock alignments or
artifact concentrations in such areas would naturally tend
to be blurred or destroyed.

The destructive power of waves on slopes is most
clearly shown at AZ T:13:31, a site on a knoll that was just
awash during the 1980 peak. Once, the site had two to three
large rock circles. At the time of this study, one circle
remained, sawed in half by a cut bank.

4. "Reservoir-specific" factors. These can be defined as those
    aspects of water control or use which are specific to each
    reservoir (see Lenihan and others 1977: 23). In the case
    of Painted Rock, the key reservoir-specific factor is its
    use as a temporary storage place for floodwaters. If water
    levels were kept fairly constant (or at least within a
    limited range), wave action (whose effect is not deeper than
    the length of the wave--Garrison 1975: 10) would only affect
    sites at that level. However, since the Painted Rock water
    level fluctuates so markedly--as floodwaters are trapped and
    then released--the whole reservoir area is subjected to
    mechanical disturbance.

    The reality of this statement is made clear by
reference to major episodes of flood control by Painted Rock
Dam as related by Troy Leatherwood and the Corps of
Engineers (1975). In 1965 and 1966, the first major flood
occurred since the dam was completed; a peak of 585.9 feet
was reached in January 1966. Release took about three
months. This flood was not great enough to affect the study
area, though it came within a few vertical feet of the area.

    A second flood peaked in May 1973, at a height of
601.3 feet. The reservoir did not fully empty until October
1976, allowing substantial opportunities for wave action.
This episode did affect some sites in the southern part of
the study area; subsequent flooding covered most of the
area.

    According to records at Painted Rock Dam, flooding
began again in March 1978; a peak of 598.1 feet occurred in
the same month. Water levels dropped slowly until December
1978, when new floods began. Peaks of 613.0 feet (January
1979), 634.7 feet (February 1979), 640.5 feet (April 1979),
and 642.3 feet (April 1979) were reached. Water levels then
dropped again until the following year, when new floods sent
the water level to a record high of 647.8 feet (March 1980).
Water levels once again dropped until December 1980, when
the reservoir was emptied. No further flooding had occurred
as of August 1981.

    It is clear that water levels are likely to range
throughout the height of the reservoir. This conclusion is
reinforced by the Corps of Engineers' (1975) simulation of
water levels in Painted Rock Reservoir, using streamflow
data from 1905 through 1975. Given the same climatic regime
over the next 70 years, we could confidently expect about a
dozen major flooding episodes, with substantial fluctuation
in water levels between 580 feet and 640 feet. We must
conclude that under current operating procedures, and given
enough time, wave action will be sufficient to destroy
every site below 661 feet in the study area.

5. Shoreline orientation. The study area is on the "north shore" of the reservoir; southerly winds prevail in the region. It is possible, therefore, that wave damage is less pronounced in areas less exposed to cross-lake winds. We have no data on this but suggest it as a possible topic for future management-oriented research. "Micro" differences in orientation, incidentally, do not seem to make much difference in terms of wave action. The north or "protected" side of rises in the area had been as badly eroded as the southern sides.

6. Siltation. This turned out not to be a problem. A little silt may have been deposited on areas below about 600 feet (including the Gila floodplain), but above that level little or no deposition was noted.

Specific Recommendations

Among the options to be considered for each cultural resource are (1) protective or management measures to protect cultural resources (2) no action and (3) excavation or relocation of the cultural resources. However, relocation of the resources would destroy their archaeological value; changes in floodwater management are out of the question; and no protective measure would prevent long-term destruction of resources by wave action or flooding. Our recommendations, therefore, fall into three remaining categories, depending on the resource in question. These are (a) no further action (b) management measures (in the form of a monitoring and testing program) and (c) surface collection or excavation of threatened resources (see Table 6.1).

Specific recommendations include:

1. The following finds are above the 661-foot floodline and will not be affected by reservoir operation: AZ T:13:26; AZ T:13:28; AZ T:13:29; PRI-13 through 15; PRI-37 through 42; PRI-44, 45, 49, and 50; PRI-53 through 62; PRI-64 through 72; and PRI-75, 77, and 80. No further action is needed unless shore areas are developed for recreation or other use.
2. Of the remaining finds, the following are probably less than 50 years old and therefore are not archaeologically significant: PRI-22, 26 through 29, and 34. No further action is needed.
3. Of the remaining finds, the following consist of three or fewer artifacts not associated with other cultural remains: PRI-3, 17, 21, 31, 36, 47, 48, 52, 73, 74, 78, and 79. It is unlikely that any additional information would be obtained by restudy of such items. No further action is recommended.

llll

444

44

4. The following sites are probably not in immediate danger of destruction: AZ T:13:22; AZ T:13:27; and PRI-2, 11, 16, 18, 19, 20, 24, 30, 32, 33, 35, 46, 51, and 76. However, repeated inundation will eventually seriously affect these sites, with rate of destruction determined by the frequency, level, and duration of floods. For these sites, we recommend a program of monitoring combined with limited testing.

The purpose of the monitoring program would be to ascertain the rate of disturbance to sites. Not all sites would have to be monitored; a representative sample would be sufficient. The following sample should be adequate: 10 features and three trail segments at AZ T:13:22 (including all artifacts within 15 m), and five other sites from among those just listed (including PRS-23).

Monitoring would begin by selecting and relocating the features and sites to be monitored. These would then be compared to previous site records, and additional records would be made as needed. Each feature should be photographed from several angles, including detail shots, to allow evaluation of rock movement. Finally, each site or feature selected should be marked with a datum, to allow relocation after subsequent episodes of flooding. (The datum should be of a noncorrosive, nonfloating material; we found that 2-foot lengths of 2-inch PVC pipe could be set quickly with a posthole digger.)

After each major flooding episode at Painted Rock, a crew would relocate and photograph the features in question. The crew would also take notes on any damage since the previous inspections, and probable cause of that damage. If no significant damage was noted, no further action would be needed until the next major episode of flooding. If, however, significant deterioration of the monitored sites was apparent, a mitigation program for the sites just listed would be needed.

We recommend that this program include limited testing. First, there is a need to assess the effects of flooding and salt cedar root growth on feature interiors and exteriors. Are occupation floors present, and if so, how badly have they been damaged? Second, excavation may clear up ambiguities about the cultural affiliation of the types of features present. Resolution of these two issues will aid the Corps in deciding on the most appropriate course of action vis-a-vis the resources in the study area.

The testing program would involve excavation of five features representing a range of sizes and forms; these should include either Feature 2 or Feature 3 (rock rings with clearly disturbed interiors). Emphasis should be on recovering culturally or temporally diagnostic materials, identifying internal or external occupation surfaces (if present), and assessing inundation damage to the feature. It should be possible to do such testing without entirely destroying the features.

5. The following sites have been heavily damaged by flooding or
    will suffer significant further damage in subsequent
    episodes of flooding: AZ T:13:23; AZ T:13:24; AZ T:13:25; AZ
    T:13:31; and PRI-5, 7, 8, 10, and 25. In addition, AZ
    T:13:30--which so far has escaped inundation--is likely to
    be severely affected by any inundation episode over 648
    feet.

All these sites are on slopes or rises, which heightens their
vulnerability to wave action. Conceivably, one more flooding episode
could destroy them. For this reason, we recommend surface collection or
excavation of these sites.

The following finds should be surface collected, with
appropriate controls: AZ T:13:23; AZ T:13:24; and PRI 5, 7, 8, and 25.
AZ T:13:23 includes several rock alignments, but the heavy damage it has
sustained makes it likely that surface collection would exhaust its
remaining research potential. The other sites are superficial
concentrations of chipped stone.

The following sites should be excavated: AZ T:13:25 (the
sleeping circle and chipped stone site), AZ T:13:30 (a knoll-top site
with multiple small features), AZ T:13:31 (a knoll-top site, a chipping
station and half a rock ring remain), and PRI-10 (a hearth with
fire-cracked rock).

Probable field time for the proposed mitigation program (setting
up the monitoring program, surface collection, and excavation) is 72
person-days. Subsequent monitoring operations (once after each major
flooding episode) would require two days for a crew of two, or a total
of 4 person-days. A detailed breakdown of the proposed program costs is
presented in Appendix C.

REFERENCES

Berge, Dale L.
    1968   The Gila Bend stage station. The Kiva 33(4):169-243.

Brown, David E., and Charles E. Lowe
    1974   A digitized computer-compatible classification for natural
            and potential vegetation in the Southwest, with particular
            reference to Arizona. Journal of the Arizona Academy of
            Science 9, supplement 2.

Carrell, Toni, Sandra Rayl, and Dan Lenihan
    1976   A literature search on the effects of fresh water inundation
            on archaeological sites through reservoir construction (draft
            copy). USDI, National Park Service, Southwest Region,
            Division of Cultural Resources. On file at Western
            Archeological Center, Tucson.

Corps of Engineers
    1975   Draft report on release-salinity study for Painted Rock Dam.
            U.S. Army Corps of Engineers, Army Engineer District, Los
            Angeles.

Garrison, E. G.
    1975   A qualitative model for inundation studies for archaeological
            research and resource conservation. Plains Anthropologist
            20:279-296.

General Accounting Office
    1981   Comptroller General's Report to the Chairman, Committee on
            Interior and Insular Affairs, House of Representatives: Are
            Agencies Doing Enough or Too Much for Archaeological
            Preservation? Washington.

Greenleaf, J. Cameron
    1975   The Fortified Hill site near Gila Bend, Arizona. The Kiva
            40(4):213-282.

Hammond, Gawain, and Norman Hammond
    1981   Child's play: a distorting factor in archaeological
            distribution. American Antiquity 46:634-636.

Hayden, Julian D.
    1972   Hohokam petroglyphs of the Sierra Pinacate, Sonora, and the
            Hohokam shell expeditions. The Kiva 37:74-83.

144   References

Irwin-Williams, Cynthia
   1979   Post-Pleistocene archaeology, 7000-2000 B.C.   In Handbook of
          North American Indians, Vol. 9, edited by Alonso Ortiz, pp.
          31-42.   Washington: Smithsonian Institution.

Johnson, Alfred E., and William W. Wasley
   1961   Pottery and artifact provenience data from sites in the
          Painted Rocks reservoir, western Arizona.   Archives of
          Archaeology 18.   Madison: University of Wisconsin Press and
          Society for American Archaeology.

Lenihan, Daniel J., Toni L. Carrell, Thomas S. Hopkins, and others
   1977   The preliminary report of the national reservoir inundation
          study.   USDI, National Park Service, Southwest Cultural
          Resources Center, Santa Fe.

Lowe, Charles H.
   1964   Arizona's Natural Environment: Landscapes and Habitats.
          Tucson: University of Arizona Press.

Martin, Paul S.
   1963   The Last 10,000 Years: A Fossil Pollen Record of the
          American Southwest.   Tucson: University of Arizona Press.

Schroeder, Albert H.
   1967   Comments on salvage archaeology in the Painted Rocks
          Reservoir, western Arizona.   Arizona Archaeologist 1:1-10.

   1979   Prehistory: Hakataya.   In Handbook of North American
          Indians, Vol. 9, edited by Alonso Ortiz, pp. 100-107.
          Washington: Smithsonian Institution.

Spier, Leslie
   1933   Yuman Tribes of the Gila River.   Chicago: University of
          Chicago Press.

Teague, Lynn S.
   1981   Test excavations at Painted Rock Reservoir: sites AZ Z:1:7,
          AZ Z:1:8, and AZ S:16:36.   Archaeological Series 143.
          Tucson: Arizona State Museum, University of Arizona.

Teague, Lynn S., and Anne R. Baldwin
   1978   Painted Rock Reservoir project, phase I: preliminary survey
          and recommendations.   Archaeological Series 126.   Tucson:
          Arizona State Museum, University of Arizona.

Van Devender, Thomas R.
   1977   Holocene woodlands in the southwestern deserts.   Science
          198:189-192.

Vogler, Lawrence E.
    1976   Cultural resources of Painted Rock Dam and Reservoir:
            preliminary evaluation and management plan recommendations.
            Archaeological Series 99. Tucson: Arizona State Museum,
            University of Arizona.

Wallace, William J.
    1978   Post-Pleistocene archaeology, 9000 to 2000 B.C. In Handbook
            of North American Indians, Vol. 8, edited by Robert F.
            Heizer, pp. 25-36. Washington: Smithsonian Institution.

Warren, Claude N.
    1967   The San Dieguito Complex: a review and hypothesis. American
            Antiquity 32:168-185.

Wasley, William W.
    1960   A Hohokam platform mound at the Gatlin site, Gila Bend, Az.
            American Antiquity 26:242-262.

Wasley, William W., and Alfred E. Johnson
    1965   Salvage archaeology in Painted Rock Reservoir, western
            Arizona. Anthropological Papers of the University of
            Arizona 9. Tucson: University of Arizona Press.